384.55
SHA

086874

RETHINKING GOVERNANCE
AND ACCOUNTABILITY

D0755315

RETHINKING GOVERNANCE AND ACCOUNTABILITY

Edited by
COLIN SHAW

BFI PUBLISHING

85874

First published in 1993 by the
British Film Institute
21 Stephen Street
London W1P 1PL

Copyright © British Film Institute 1993

British Library Cataloguing-in-Publication Data.
A catalogue record for this book is available from the
British Library.

ISBN 0-85170-426-3

Cover design: Romas Foord

Typeset in 10/11½ pt Sabon by
Goodfellow & Egan Phototypesetting Ltd, Cambridge

Printed in Great Britain by
St Edmundsbury Press,
Bury St Edmunds, Suffolk

Contents

Notes on Contributors

Eric M. Barendt is Goodman Professor of Media Law at University College London.

Roger Gale is Member of Parliament for North Thanet.

Nicholas Garnham is Director of the Centre for Communication and Information Studies.

Christopher Hood is Professor of Public Administration at the London School of Economics.

Graham Mather is President of the European Policy Forum.

Colin Shaw is Director of the Broadcasting Standards Council.

Michael Stevenson is Secretary of the BBC.

Phillip Whitehead is Chairman of the Consumers' Association.

Preface

The BBC is central to the cultural life of Britain. It is one of the major British success stories of the post-war period. It is renowned for its public service ideals. It is recognised throughout the world as a producer of quality programming and for its impartial news coverage. But the emerging technologies in broadcasting and telecommunications have thrown this history of achievement into sharp relief: the television landscape is changing irreversibly in Britain and across the rest of the world as competition becomes the norm and regulation is deemed less necessary in a world of multiple channels. How should the BBC change as an institution in the face of all these factors? What are the most important areas which need to be considered ahead of the renewal of the BBC's Royal Charter of 1996?

The British Film Institute is not likely to be directly affected by the outcome of the debate on the BBC, but we see it as a major part of our work to ensure that the debates which flow from the Charter renewal process are brought to as wide an audience as possible. This Charter Review series seeks to address the major issues outlined in the Government's consultation document. We have commissioned authors from a variety of political perspectives to explore the key questions. Each contribution is the expression of the author's viewpoint and does not reflect BFI policy. Indeed the BFI has submitted its own response to the Government alongside the many other interested organisations and individuals.

We hope each of the books in this series will lead to a more focused debate. The BBC's own documents *Extending Choice* and the subsequent *Responding to the Green Paper* contain essentially pragmatic formulations. This may well be the most appropriate position to take in a world replete with uncertainties. However, there are alternatives, particularly in the much disputed area of the future governance of the BBC which is the subject of this book, and we wish to see these debated. We hope that readers will find ideas in these pages and in this series which stimulate their thinking about these issues, and, if so, we will feel we have succeeded.

Geoff Mulgan and Richard Paterson
Series Editors
August 1993

Introduction

COLIN SHAW

Dame Edith Evans, it is said, did not take kindly on one occasion to the presence of a young and inexperienced director. When, after a rehearsal, she had brushed aside his suggestion that she might like to have some notes from him on her performance, he asked plaintively what he was expected to do. She replied, with wicked charity, 'Don't worry, my dear, I shall think of something for you.'

The BBC's Board of Governors, it has sometimes appeared, are in the position of the young director. It is necessary for them to be there, but what they should be asked to do is a matter of speculation. This monograph is concerned with attempts to find answers to the speculation.

The broadsheets remind us almost daily that, in Britain, we are facing a crisis in authority. Yeats's non-holding centre has been invoked a thousand times over. In the last five years the crisis in broadcasting has grown steadily more acute. The 1990 Broadcasting Act, directed principally, but by no means exclusively, at the commercial sector is steadily being revealed in its true colours, threatening to make a mockery of the meaning of the word 'choice', the defining purpose so often paraded while the bill was being debated. In such a situation, the need to preserve the public service sector of British broadcasting grows more urgent if a broad range of programmes of high quality is to be sustained.

The principle of intervention in the public interest in the spending proposals of broadcasters, which lies at the heart of public service broadcasting, does not automatically require the existence of the licence fee or predicate the continuance of the BBC. But none of the alternative methods of funding or the creation of new institutions seem sufficiently attractive to encourage the replacement at present either of the licence fee as the main source of financing the BBC or of the BBC itself. Only one of the essays which follow suggests that the BBC might disappear.

1

In considering the order in which the essays should appear, it seemed to me that we should begin with Christopher Hood's account of the Corporation's position within the developing history of modern institutions. He makes clear the increasingly anomalous constitution of the BBC in a society where the disciplines of the market have become accepted more and more as the right and only tests of an institution's success. Although in *Extending Choice* and its sequel, *Responding to the Green Paper*, the BBC's Governors and their senior employees strive hard to adopt the jargon and practices of the marketplace, the many-sided nature of their product – services of programmes which collectively attempt to match ideals of public service – frequently jars with their strivings.

Nicholas Garnham's essay follows as a complement to the first essay, further exploring the history of pressure for accountability in British broadcasting. Towards his conclusion, however, Professor Garnham proposes a set of alternatives to the existing structures of the BBC, reflecting his belief that to leave things as they are 'would be a Pyrrhic victory'.

The next two essays focus attention particularly on the audience, the consumers of broadcasting. Roger Gale paints a depressing picture of the BBC's future in a world where multichannel television is available in every home and asks whether, in such circumstances, the interests of the consumer will truly be served. Phillip Whitehead is in no doubt that it is to its audiences that the BBC needs to be accountable. He looks forward to a redefining of the Governors' tasks and the creation of a consumers' organisation as steps towards a greater degree of accountability.

In his essay, Graham Mather explores the value of the proposal, fostered by the Chairman of the ITC, Sir George Russell, for a single body overseeing all British television, but rejects it on the grounds that there would be too many conflicts of interest. That would not rule out, in his view, closer co-operation between the regulators of the commercial sector and a restyled body of regulators for the public service sector. Mr Mather also raises the question of how Governors are appointed, a consideration discussed in my own essay, which urges the greater separation of the Board of Governors from the management of the BBC, enabling them to perform their role as trustees of the public interest more effectively.

The essay by Professor Barendt debates the possibility of reconstituting the BBC by statute rather than by renewing the Royal Charter which, in contrast to a statute, runs only for a fixed period.

The final essay, by Michael Stevenson, records the Governors' own answer to the initial question, 'What are the Governors to do?', and

2

provides some responses to a number of the solutions put forward by the other essayists. By fortunate accident, this monograph is going to press shortly after the BBC's 1992/3 Annual Review (no longer the Report of old) has appeared, reflecting in practice the distinctions between Governors and management of which Mr Stevenson has written.

In introducing these essays to their readers, let me recall that Michael Swann, when he was Chairman of the BBC in the mid-70s, defined the role of the Governors as to challenge the orthodoxies of the professionals. His words are a useful reminder that there are philosophical and moral issues which should remain at least as heavy a charge on the shoulders of Trustee-Governors as the successful pursuit of performance indicators or the measurement of efficiency.

In conclusion, I cannot do better than echo the words of Wilf Stevenson in his introduction to the first of the series. He said that there can be few blueprints emerging from any debate of current broadcasting issues. The task is to find one which will sustain the public service sector so that it can continue to enrich the broadcasting services available to the people of Britain, whoever and wherever they are.

The BBC: An Island of Progressivism in a Sea of New Public Management[1]

CHRISTOPHER HOOD

Introduction: A Progressive-Era Design

As an institution the BBC is now as much a period piece as a 20s crystal set or valve radio. Its organisational architecture follows the design principles of a vanished era. That design comes from the age of 'progressivism' in which radio broadcasting first began to develop, and reflects the values of public administration prevailing at that time.

Most contemporary theorists of 'public management' notably David Osborne and Ted Gaebler in their bestseller, *Reinventing Government*,[2] claim that progressivism is no longer relevant to the provision of most public services today. Can their general argument be applied to the organisation of broadcasting in the United Kingdom?

This brief chapter, written by a student of public administration ideas rather than a broadcasting specialist, has four main parts. First, it identifies what progressives argued for in public administration and why. Second, it looks at the way broadcasting relates to progressive concerns. Third, it suggests that the general trend in public administration, both in the United Kingdom and in many other OECD countries, has been running against 'progressive' doctrines in the recent past. Fourth, and finally, it argues that, contrary to the general claims of Osborne and Gaebler, progressive concerns cannot be wholly dismissed from the public administration of broadcasting even today. But as an institutional arrangement the BBC represents only one possible 'progressive' response to the problem. Its current boundaries are difficult to defend from a progressive logic. And other tools of progressivism, perhaps in modified form, may be just as important in making broadcasting more effective in investigating and exposing abuses of high public offices.

The Essence of Progressive-Era Public Administration: Two Design Principles

Progressive public administration embodied two cardinal principles.

4

One was that the public sector should as far as possible be kept distinct from the private sector. Public servants should form a 'Jesuitical corps', a favourite and recurring metaphor, used by Beatrice Webb and others.[3] Service in such a corps was seen as a principled and ascetic calling, to be kept highly distinct from the general run of private business in matters of recruitment, ethos, reward, promotion and organisational structure. Only by strictly insulating the public sector from the methods, and the morals, of the private sector could corruption be kept in check, capture avoided and able and educated people attracted to responsible careers at fairly low rates of pay compared to their private sector counterparts. Hence the importance of staffing the public service with, to use the famous opening words of the Northcote–Trevelyan report of 1854, '*permanent* officers ... possessing ... *independence, character*, ability and experience' (author's italics).[4]

The other distinctive design principle of progressive public administration was to restrict the 'hands-on' power of those at the top, elected politicians and appointed chief executives alike. That power was to be sharply limited by a battery of procedural rules and the establishment of semi-independent institutions operating as 'public sector trusts' (in words used by Keynes in 1952).[5] They were to pursue the public interest in relative autonomy from politicians, free from the various temptations that elected political flesh is heir to. And a battery of restrictive rules, mostly on the letting of contracts and decisions over staffing, would ensure that any discretionary power was not abused by those at the top in hiring and promoting their friends or favourites while passing over outsiders or those with independent views.

Nowadays these traditional principles of institutional design are more often derided than explained sympathetically. But although the ideas are unfashionable, they are not incoherent, and they are at the very least an intelligible response to a particular historical context. Progressive public administration is most often associated with the 'clean government' movement that developed in the United States in the late 19th and early 20th centuries, and Woodrow Wilson's famous ideas in 1887 about separating 'professional' administration from party political spoils.[6] But somewhat similar doctrines developed in the United Kingdom, for example, in the ideas of Fabian public administration and in what Rosamund Thomas calls 'the British philosophy of administration'[7] developed by a group of turn-of-the-century civil servants and LSE dons. In Australia, too, progressivism exerted a strong influence on administrative design, particularly in the development of 'strong' statutory boards relatively independent of cabinets and central agencies of government, both at state and Commonwealth levels.[8]

Progressive ideas emerged in an era when the extension of the franchise coincided with the concentration of business and the development of organised crime. Markets came to be dominated by a few large corporations, increasing the political power of those corporations as lobbyists, contractors and electoral campaign contributors. The rise of organised crime in the cities, at least in the United States, added another element of monopoly and power over individual citizens.

In these conditions the professional middle classes feared that the machine politicians produced by the extended franchise would engender cowed, corrupt and incompetent public bureaucracies. Democracy was seen to be threatened by ever-more concentrated corporate power and the power of organised crime. Hence the criminal and corporate sectors needed to be checked by independent public institutions whose decisions or activities were not available for sale by corruptible vote-seeking politicians. Devices of popular referendum, initiative and recall were also part of the standard progressive recipe for checking corruption among politicians by limiting their legislative power and making it possible for them to be removed from office outside normal election periods.[9]

Hence the separation of the public service from the private sector was seen as a bulwark against crime and corruption, and power-limiting procedural rules and independent public institutions were conceived as a means of limiting harassment, favouritism and abuse of office by those in high official positions, whether elected or appointed. The notion was that such an institutional design would deliver not only honest government, something taken as a value in itself, but also cheaper government, since it was held that the 'cost of government was directly proportional to the dishonesty of politicians'.[10] Obtaining public services by franchise, contract or auction was not seen as an automatic recipe for economy and quality in conditions where 'markets' were increasingly dominated by a few larger corporations (if not by organised crime) and accessible only through politicians who needed campaign contributions to finance their ever-more expensive electoral machines.

As a logic of organisational design, progressive public administration can be understood in several ways. Culturally it is clearly an embodiment of 'hierarchist' attitudes.[11] The public sector is to be a 'group' highly distinct from the private and criminal sector, with its transactions governed by a complex 'grid' of rules and institutional arrangements. As a control system, progressivism relies on the entrenchment of rival contradictory values in semi-independent institutions rather than simple target-setting and monitoring from a single controlling centre.[12] As an incentive system, the progressive model has

6

three main features. First, it takes the basic contract relationship in public sector organisations as one of trustee and beneficiary rather than the now more conventional economic theory metaphor of principal and agent. Second, it relies on long-term, high-trust contracting rather than short-term, low-trust contracting.[13] Implicitly the notion is that concerns with long-term reputation (rather than with short-term monetary gains and losses) will check opportunism, shirking and slack within the public sector. Third, it rests on the assumption that contracting for public services faces particular difficulties. These difficulties include not only market concentration (and associated contracting problems like 'first mover advantage' and bargaining deadlocks), but also illegal pressures and practices.

The Relevance of Progressivism to Broadcasting

The development of broadcasting produced a particular challenge to progressivism. The public policy debate over broadcasting ranges over many issues. It embraces debates about the maintenance of 'national identity' and culture (including different national identities and multiculturalism); support for the arts, education, trailblazing and standard-setting. But, at least viewed through progressive public administration spectacles, the 'national identity' argument and the 'Covent Garden' argument for maintenance of elite culture are not of the essence. The key constitutional issue was (and remains) whether broadcasting would be an instrument of 'big government' or a check on it.

Therefore the central issue from this perspective is not efficiency in a narrow sense, but who is to control broadcast comment, scrutiny and investigation. Broadcast journalism could potentially offer a power check on political corruption and abuse of high public office by bringing such abuse directly to the attention of the mass audience. Potentially it offered a radically new dimension to Jeremy Bentham's famous precepts about the need for 'transparency' in government, and the 'goldfish bowl' conditions which he advocated for the conduct of all public affairs (using the well-known maxim that 'the more closely we are watched, the better we behave'). In principle it could be a 'pantopticon' for government itself.

Who controlled that potential and under what conditions clearly raised issues at the heart of the concerns of progressive public administration. Direct 'hands-on' political control (for example, through a government department headed by a minister) would greatly enhance the power of those in high public office, if only by denying the use of the medium to their critics. Operation through an unregulated private market, on the other hand, offered the risk that

7

the broadcasting organisations would be bought and operated by crooks or fanatics (to whom they would, naturally, have the most value). It also offered the risk that commercial pressures would make investigative journalists avoid expensive 'big dip' inquiries into public and private misconduct and that such considerations would expose them to self-censorship and proprietorial pressures to keep out of political trouble.

Hence progressivism would firmly reject both hands-on political control and unregulated private market control for broadcasting. That leaves them with three basic institutional options for handling the commentary and investigative functions of broadcasting.[14] One is what might be called the 'Bundesbank' solution: monopoly public provision through a national or regional public enterprise structure endowed with sufficient independence in finance and decision-making power to challenge government effectively. A second, is 'metaphytic', or public-private competition, the traditional Australian progressive-era formula for 'keeping them honest' in business and politics.[15] A third is private ownership more or less heavily regulated by independent institutions, a distinctive feature of the American progressive style of public administration.

All of these institutional approaches have been used in the United Kingdom. Here the original stress was on 'information, education and entertainment' (rather than exposure and investigation of abuse of office) as the central role of public service broadcasting. But it set broadcasting broadly within a progressive public administration framework, originally in the form of the 'Bundesbank' model described above. Hence the BBC's Royal Charter (rather than statutory incorporation), the special tax base and the other trappings of relative independence with which the BBC has been endowed as a public institution.

Less than thirty years later (indeed after only about twenty years of actual peacetime operation) the other two models came to be used, with independent regulation of the provision of private programme services through the ITA (later the IBA) and the pattern of public-private competition initiated by the 1954 Television Act and subsequent legislation, first in television and then in radio. Interestingly the progressivist potential of broadcasting in laying government open to independent scrutiny and exposure only developed in this later era, and some of the private companies took up this role as well as (if not more so than) the BBC. The issue for the 90s is essentially how far *any* progressivist design can or should remain in this area, and, if so, what mix of the options is appropriate.

8

Table 1 NPM as a Challenge to Progressive Public Administration

	No.	Doctrine	Assumed link to performance	Replaces	Operational significance
PS Distinctiveness	1	'Unbundle' the public service into corporatised units organised by product	Make units 'manageable'; focus blame; create anti-waste lobby by splitting provision & production	Belief that public service needs to be uniform & inclusive to be accountable without underlaps & overlaps	Erosion of single service employment; arm's-length dealings; devolved budgets
	2	More contract-based competitive provision, with internal markets and term contracts	Rivalry will cut costs & push up standards; contracts will make performance standards explicit	Flexibility, independence & lower transaction costs require loosely specified employment contracts & open-ended provision	Distinction of primary & secondary public service labour force
	3	Stress on private sector styles of management practice	Need to apply 'proven' private sector management tools in the public sector	Stress on public service 'ethic'; fixed pay & hiring rules; model employer stance; centralised staffing structure, jobs for life	Move from double imbalance PS pay, career service, unmonetised rewards, 'due process' employee entitlements
Rules vs Discretion	5	Put more emphasis on visible 'hands-on' top management	Accountability requires clear assignment of responsibility not diffusion of power	Paramount stress on policy skills & rules, not active management	More 'freedom to manage' by discretionary power
	6	Make performance standards & measures explicit, formal & measurable	Accountability means clearly stated aims; efficiency needs 'hard look' at goals	Qualitative & implicit standards and norms	Erosion of self-management by professionals
	7	Greater emphasis on output controls	Need for greater stress on results	Stress on procedure & control by 'collibration' (opposed maximisers)	Resources & pay based on performance; blurring of funds for pay & activity

Source: adapted from C. C. Hood, 'A public management for all seasons?', *Public Administration* 69, 1991, pp. 4–5

The General Challenge to Progressivism

The progressive public administration design to which the BBC originally belongs is waning across many of the OECD countries, though not all of them.[16] Current doctrines of 'New Public Management' or 'Reinventing Government' (in Osborne and Gaebler's phrase)[17] go clean counter to the two cardinal design principles of progressivism as described earlier.

In place of the progressive preference for insulation of the public sector from the private sector, New Public Management aims for 'entrepreneurial bureaucracies' using the methods and style of the private sector to get results. And in place of the progressive preference for rules and independent public organisations to check the power of those in high public office, New Public Management aims to strengthen the hands-on capacity of managers to direct their organisations without being hamstrung by restrictive legislation. At the same time, the twilight of progressivism, at least in some countries, seems to entail a weakening of independent public organisations relative to central agencies and cabinets.[18]

The specific doctrines of New Public Management are now familiar, and need no description here. For convenience they are set out in Table 1 and simplified into six basic doctrines, with an indication of the progressive-style doctrines which they replace. Three of the doctrines relate to the distinctiveness of the public sector and three relate to the extent of the rules or independent institutions limiting central discretion.

In the first of these two new dimensions New Public Management favours 'unbundling' large public sector organisations into corporatised units organised by product, splitting purchaser and provider. It favours more contract-based competitive provision, with internal markets and term contracts. It favours a shift towards private sector styles of management practice, applying 'proven' private sector management tools (such as pay for performance) in the public sector instead of a distinctive public service ethics and method of doing business.

In the second dimension, New Public Management favours a shift towards a greater emphasis on hands-on management by those at the top; it favours more explication of standards of success and performance, replacing an earlier emphasis on qualitative and implicit standards and goals. It favours more stress on 'results', with less emphasis placed on control by procedure and the entrenchment of particular output controls with an accompanying greater emphasis on them.

These familiar New Public Management doctrines essentially represent a different conception of 'accountability' from that embodied in

10

progressive public administration. The word 'accountability' in New Public Management thinking reflects a 'principal-agent' model, related to economic theory in the 60s and 70s about the design of optimal incentive payments in the face of managerial discretion in business firms.[19] It is used to mean narrow specification of performance standards set or agreed by 'principals' and monitored from a controlling centre. In order for there to be accountability, to this way of thinking, it must be possible to identify 'managers' with discretionary power over each provision unit as the sources of praise or blame.

For progressive public administration, on the other hand, accountability requires that the structure of public administration be comprehensible and intelligible to citizens at large, limiting underlaps and overlaps rather than parcelling out responsibility to a large number of public sector providers. Moreover accountability for progressive public administration is seen less in terms of 'principals' and 'agents' than of 'trustees and beneficiaries'. There is a big difference between these two accountability metaphors. 'Trustees' are not directly accountable to a 'principal' and, at most, only indirectly accountable to the beneficiaries whom they serve (not even indirectly, when the beneficiary is an animal or a monument). Rather than with reference to the specific goals of the beneficiaries, breach of trust is essentially defined in *procedural* shortcomings, notably with reference to the trustees' failure to put the beneficiaries' interests first, to act diligently on their behalf and to observe the conditions of the trust deed.

Is the Progressive Approach Relevant to Broadcasting Today?
Many of the doctrines of New Public Management (such as unbundling and producer–purchaser splits) have found their way into the internal management of the BBC. The Director-General's tax-efficient 'commercial' pay arrangement which came to light in March 1993 is a well-publicised case of the importation of private sector practices into the public sector, replacing an earlier standardised approach to employment. The debates over such changes follow the general lines of argument about the respective merits of progressivism and managerialism. But the BBC's internal management arrangements are only a relatively small part of the larger issue of the relevance of progressivism to the organisation of broadcasting in the 90s.

There are strong grounds for claiming that broadcasting remains an area in which the preoccupations of progressive public administration, briefly outlined in Table 1, are particularly relevant. The case for independent public power in broadcast journalism seems at least as strong as the case for independent central banks or public audit offices, because the currency at stake also involves issues of long-term trust. From this viewpoint the comment and scrutiny functions of broadcasting are not just a bread-and-butter service to be delivered by producer agencies to defined customers or users according to relatively simple criteria. Rather, independent and critical media are a precondition for honesty in the media as a whole.

Moreover it does not seem plausible to argue that, in general, the risks of degradation to public life which are posed by the power of big business corporations, big crime and the potential abuse of public office are any less serious today than they were in the 20s. The central weakness of Osborne and Gaebler's recipe for 'reinventing government'[20] is the way that it largely ignores such problems. Further, the view that the United Kingdom in particular should for some reason be inherently and permanently immune to the sort of serious abuse of high public office which has recently come to light in other wealthy democracies (for example, Japan, Australia, Italy and the United States) seems dangerously complacent. Indeed the more that the United Kingdom, in line with New Public Management doctrines, moves away from progressive style, the more important it becomes for there to be strong independent checks on political and business corruption, to police the existing frontier between the private and the public sector. The United Kingdom has nothing comparable with the Hong Kong anticorruption commissions or their Australian equivalents, and hence there is a much larger scrutiny vacuum for broadcasting to fill.

However, such concerns do not necessarily justify the present boundaries of the BBC, whose operation involves many activities which are much more in the nature of simple service delivery (for example, screening old movies). Such services do not involve the same extent of inescapable fiduciary and adversarial behaviour as the scrutiny and comment function, and perhaps can be performed just as well under the conditions of New Public Management. Indeed taking a progressive perspective seriously would suggest a critical scrutiny of the BBC's current range of functions, which have grown by accumulation over the years rather than according to any strict progressive logic. It might suggest a smaller organisation with a sharper scrutiny mandate, not simply to operate honestly, but actively to seek to expose dishonesty.

It is also highly debatable from the BBC's track record how far the organisation has actually lived up to its progressive design as an independent force in constitutional life. It is no Bundesbank. As a counterweight to corruption, its record in helping to put errant British politicians and business tycoons behind bars is hardly impressive. Its investigative activities have never brought down a government, and in fact it is doubtful whether it has exposed those in high public office to a greater degree of critical scrutiny than the private broadcasting companies or the print media over recent decades. It has done nothing that even comes close to matching the Australian Broadcasting Commission's damning exposure of public corruption in Queensland in its famous *Moonlight State* documentary in 1987, ultimately leading to the downfall of the Bjeklke–Peterson regime.[21]

Whether the BBC could ever perform effective scrutiny on abuse of office with the current range of activities which has developed and which depend on the licence tax is debatable. Advertising, a small range of functions financed by the licence tax or even a transnational consortium might be required to achieve enough independence from national government to expose abuse of office effectively. It may be, too, that more effective guarantees of freedom of speech, including less restrictive libel laws, might be needed to create the conditions for all broadcasters to investigate and expose dishonesty more readily (though it may be noted that Australian libel laws are at least as strict as those in the United Kingdom, but did not prevent the broadcasting of *Moonlight State*).

The BBC's record suggests that a 'public trust' broadcasting corporation is not the only, or even the best, way to provide checks on those in high public office that the concerns of progressive public administration would require. Indeed it could be argued that there are distinct dangers in relying on any one institution to provide such checks. After all, it is far from unknown for public organisations to undermine the very values which they were originally set up to promote.[22] Even if such a 'self-destruct' fate is avoided, the independence of an institution becomes more 'dignified' than 'efficient' (in Walter Bagehot's famous terms) and any 'public trust' must be vulnerable to such a fate.

Hence the other two progressive public administration recipes mentioned earlier, the independent regulator and the public-private competition models, may be as effective, or even more so, as the unaided efforts of an independent public corporation in checking abuses of high public office. Undoubtedly there are major difficulties with independent regulation in an age of close substitutes for traditional broadcasting (cable, satellite) and the permeation of national boundaries. Those who were formerly regulated are losing the *de facto* monopolies which were the quid pro quo for regulation. But the extension of the public-private frontier in New Public Management, as referred to earlier, makes it all the more important to limit control of broadcast media by the growing number of firms providing public services on contract. In that way, their activities can be independently scrutinised and exposed without conflict of interest.

In principle an institutional structure which combined the three elements of progressivism (independent public corporations, public-private competition, independent regulation) can be more robust than reliance on any single recipe. Combining the forms offers the possibility that if any one element failed, whether it were the independence of the public broadcaster, the effect of competition in encouraging mutual honesty or the power of independent regulation to check conflicts of interest, enough of the others would remain so that abuse of public office could be checked and publicised. Of course it is always possible that there would be 'common mode failure', in the language of fault tree analysis.

What would be most worrying for the progressive public administration agenda would be a position in which all of the progressive public administration recipes in the area were simultaneously weakened: for instance, in the erosion of independence in the public broadcaster, segmented markets rather than public-private competition in the scrutiny of public affairs, less stringent independent regulation of broadcasting or more hands-on regulation by politicians. General enthusiasm for what New Public Management can do to shake up many areas of torpid service delivery should not blind us to the values of progressivism in particular cases. If broadcasting has an important role in helping to expose corruption and to scrutinise the actions of those in high public office, this role requires special institutional forms, a different language for the debate than has hitherto been used and a different set of criteria for success.

Notes

1. I am grateful to Geoff Mulgan for helpful comments on an earlier version of this paper.
2. D. Osborne and T. Gaebler, *Reinventing Government* (Reading, Mass.: Addison-Wesley, 1992).
3. R. Barker, 'The Fabian state', in B. Pimlott (ed.), *Fabian Essays in Socialist Thought* (London: Heinemann, 1984), p. 34.
4. *Report on the Organization of the Permanent Civil Service, Together with a Letter from the Rev. B. Jowett*, Cmd 1713 (London: HMSO, 1854), p. 3. See also J. Nethercote, 'Public service reform', a paper presented to conference of Academy of Social Sciences of Australia on the Public Service, University House, Australian National University, 25 February 1989.
5. J. M. Keynes, *Essays in Persuasion* (London: Macmillan, 1952).
6. W. Wilson, 'The study of administration', *Political Science Quarterly* 2, 1887, pp. 197–222.

7. R. Thomas, *The British Philosophy of Administration* (London: Longman, 1978).
8. J. Halligan and R. Wettenhall, 'Major changes in the structure of government institutions', in J. Power (ed.), *Public Administration in Australia: A Watershed* (Sydney: RAIPA/Hale and Iremonger, 1990).
9. G. de Q Walker, *Initiative and Referendum: The People's Law* (Sydney: Centre for Independent Studies, 1987).
10. B. D. Karl, *Executive Reorganization and Reform in the New Deal* (Cambridge, Mass.: Harvard University Press, 1963), p. 18.
11. M. Douglas, *In the Active Voice* (London: Routledge, 1982), pp. 183–254.
12. A Dunsire, *Control in a Bureaucracy* (Oxford: Martin Robertson, 1978). See also by the same author, 'Holistic governance', *Public Policy and Administration* 5 (1), 1990, pp. 3–18.
13. A. Fox, *Beyond Contract: Work, Power and Trust Relations* (London: Faber & Faber, 1974); M. Sako, 'The role of "trust" in Japanese buyer–seller relationships', *Ricerche Economiche* 45, 1991, pp. 449–74.
14. C. C. Hood and G. F. Schuppert (eds.), *Delivering Public Services in Western Europe* (London: Sage, 1988), pp. 44–8.
15. D. Corbett, *Politics and the Airlines* (London: Allen & Unwin, 1965).
16. P. Aucoin, 'Administrative reform in public management: paradigms, principles, paradoxes and pendulums', *Governance* 3, 1990, pp. 115–37; C. C. Hood, 'Beyond the public bureaucracy state? Public administration in the 1990s', inaugural lecture, London School of Economics, 16 January 1990; C. C. Hood, 'A public management for all seasons?', *Public Administration* 69, 1991, pp. 3–19.
17. Osborne and Gaebler, *Reinventing Government*.
18. Halligan and Wettenhall, 'Changes in the structure of government institutions'.
19. H. Leibenstein, *Beyond Economic Man: A New Foundation for Micro-economics* (Cambridge, Mass.: Harvard University Press, 1976).
20. Osborne and Gaebler, *Reinventing Government*.
21. C. Masters, *Inside Story* (Sydney: Angus and Robertson, 1992).
22. M. Painter, 'Values in the history of public administration', in J. Power (ed.), *Public Administration in Australia*, pp. 75–93.

The Future of Public Service Broadcasting in Britain in Historical Perspective

NICHOLAS GARNHAM

The debate on the future of public service broadcasting occasioned by the need to renew the BBC's Charter in 1996 and initiated by the Government's Green Paper[1] and the BBC's response[2] has once again placed the question of accountability at the centre of the broadcasting policy agenda. The debate during the 80s was dominated by questions of economics and technology. The hope was that the problem of accountability, which has haunted broadcasting since its birth in the 20s, could be solved by the exercise of consumer sovereignty. The new technologies of cable and satellite would deliver choice, and consumers would then freely exercise that choice on a market for programmes. Government intervention would be confined to consumer protection. We are now, however, returning to the agenda of the 70s when accountability was last to the fore. The purpose of this essay is to revisit the policy debates of that period to see what lessons we can draw from them.

The problem of accountability is central to any public service broadcasting system because the concept of service implies a master/ servant relationship of some sort between the provider of the service and the person or group to whom it is provided. It implies the right of those being served to ensure that the service they are offered meets their needs and is provided in a manner they consider appropriate. It also entails the right to ensure that necessary changes are made in the light of their wishes.

Public service broadcasting can be defined as any broadcasting service which is not provided simply as a good in a market for private profit. To a certain degree this includes all broadcasting simply because it uses the radio spectrum, a scarce public resource, and thus its commercial freedoms are everywhere constrained to a greater or lesser extent, in the public interest, by licence obligations. It is also the case, as even that advocate of consumer sovereignty and market freedom, the Peacock Committee,[3] was forced to recognise, that

16

because of the economic peculiarities of broadcasting (consumers do not in general themselves pay directly for programmes) governments are forced to intervene to protect the consumer even when the system is privately financed and funded out of advertising revenues. To this extent it is correct for the ITC and the Radio Authority, with the broadcasting services they regulate, to claim that they, and not the BBC alone, are also public service broadcasters. It is thus difficult to confine any discussion of accountability in public service broadcasting only to the Corporation. One is inevitably driven to consider the system as a whole, as, for instance, with the current suggestion for a Public Service Broadcasting Board to allocate licence-fee revenue to anyone providing public service programmes.

However, because of the immediacy of the question of renewing the BBC's Charter, this essay will focus its discussion of accountability on the BBC, or rather on a system of broadcasting which receives funding in one form or another from the state and is not run for private profit but to deliver a broadcasting service whose aims are in some sense, however vague, publicly defined. This means that, for the purposes of the essay, we are talking about a broadcasting service for which accountability to consumers through the market, the overwhelming focus of the policy debate in the 80s, is not open as a solution to the problem of accountability.

Even when discussing the accountability of public service broadcasting in this narrow sense, a version of the consumer sovereignty model has been both popular and pervasive. It has been argued, for instance by the Annan Committee,[4] that the public knows what it is getting from watching television and listening to the radio, and that the ultimate test of a broadcasting service is the response of individual viewers and listeners to individual programmes. It is important to correct this popular, superficially attractive, but erroneous view, if only because it is so widespread, so popular with broadcasting executives and regulators alike, and because it acts, and has historically acted, as a block to coherent thought about accountability. Broadcasting is precisely a service. It is more than its sum of constituent programme parts. The quality of a broadcasting service cannot be judged, or indeed planned, as a mere string of individual programmes, but necessarily involves schedules to be judged against criteria of range, balance, sustained creative originality and value for money. It is for this reason also that broadcasting cannot easily solve its accountability problem through reliance on a market. It was for this reason that the Peacock Committee was forced to argue that such consumer sovereignty could only come into being within a system of universal pay-per-programme via broadband cable. This essay is based

17

on the assumption that such a scenario, even if achievable in the long-term, is not one which will be realised within the time scale of current broadcasting policy thinking and that therefore the problem of accountability remains to face us.

Indeed, if one examines the history of British broadcasting it is striking how consistent both the discussions of accountability and the attempts to fashion structures of accountability have been since the 20s. While the detailed emphasis may change, as the social, political and economic contexts change, the debate has been a variation on a limited number of themes and suggested institutional responses to a few key recurring problems.

The first problem is the search for an answer to the paradox of how to combine freedom for broadcasters from undesirable state control, while at the same time ensuring the necessary level of desirable political accountability. This has been a particularly thorny problem for the British system, which is founded on the absolute sovereignty of Parliament as the expression of the people's will. In practice, of course, this circle cannot be squared, so that any structure and practice of accountability has to be a balance between the two. Where at any time the balance is to be struck will remain a matter of contention, the emphasis shifting as the social, political and economic climates change. What is certain is that any debate on accountability will be unfruitful and any proposed structure unhelpful unless this unresolvable tension is recognised. The lesson of history is, in particular, that broadcasters forget at their peril the necessity of limits to their freedom. Such neglect is regularly avenged by even greater control. At the same time it should be recognised that a favourite control tactic of broadcasting managers and regulators is to persuade broadcasters not to exercise their freedom lest it is taken away from them.

The second problem is how to combine managerial efficiency with public accountability. This, indeed, was the problem which dominated discussion in the early days. It was part of a wider debate on how state enterprises should be run, since it was recognised that Civil Service procedures were not appropriate for operating agencies whose functions more closely resembled a conventional business than a government department. Here we should note that managerial efficiency can mean different things. Are we concerned with day-to-day management, the need for flexibility of response and rapid decision-taking or are we concerned with strategic management, the broad direction in which the enterprise is to go? The desirability for maximum freedom of broadcasting managers in the former field has too often been used as a smoke screen to keep the really important strategic decisions out of the reach of public scrutiny. But where the line is drawn between those executive decisions it is appropriate for the management to take independently and those which should come under the control of whatever system of accountability is instituted is a matter of the greatest importance and one on which clarity is essential. This issue about the form of the relationship between the Governors of the BBC and the BBC's Board of Management is central to the current debate.

The next problem, which has been recurrent, is how the public for whom the service is designed should make its views known. One version of accountability would argue – as it was strongly argued by the IBA at the time of Annan – that Parliament is the unique source of public accountability. The establishment of other bodies to exert public pressure on the IBA or the BBC Governors would be to undermine Parliament and indeed to introduce an illegitimate source of partial authority – the lobby group as opposed to the people.[5] This is not an argument which can be dismissed lightly. In practice, however, the exercise of such parliamentary authority through, for instance, the scrutiny of a select committee or a version of direct political representation on the Board of Governors, on the lines of the Italian or German systems, has been resisted on the grounds that it would lead to undue interference with the necessary autonomy from politics of broadcasting. This line of argument produces the *reductio ad absurdum* of the view expressed by the IBA to the Annan Committee that 'broadcasting should be responsible to the public without being answerable to its rulers'. This would result in the broadcasters being in practice unanswerable to anyone but themselves, unless the public is brought back in through a system which provides it with real powers of sanction. For as Mary Warnock, who developed the philosophical argument upon which the IBA's position was based, has argued, the power to exercise sanctions is central to any system of accountability. Since the public had no sanctions to impose on the broadcasting authorities, she contended, the authorities were not answerable to the public. The sanctions which are in the hands of governments are such, however, that they can never or hardly ever by exercised except in the broadest terms.

As we shall see, nevertheless, within a vision of the separation of powers and recognising the influence on politicians of organised expressions of public view, a recurring theme in all the discussions has been the need to construct institutional mechanisms within the broadcasting sector to express the public's views and to bring them to bear on the decision processes of politicians and/or regulators and/or broadcasting managements. Thus the Sykes Committee[6] in 1923 proposed an Independent Broadcasting Board which was 'to express the conception of public service through public representation of complaints and proposals about broadcasting direct to the Post Office', then a government department and responsible for broadcasting policy. This was never, in fact, acted upon.

The existing system of accountability for the BBC, for all its venerability and apparent stability, was the result of what Reith himself called a muddle. Its key ingredients are:

- a Board of Governors appointed by government and responsible to Parliament for running the BBC in 'the national interest'
- licence-fee finance to ensure freedom from either commercial or state financial control and to provide, however minimally, a direct financial link between the public and the broadcasting service.

Any structure of accountability for the BBC has to manage the relationship of the BBC to three constituencies – the state, the public and broadcasters. Two of this triumvirate, the state and the public, are obvious and are the main focus of this essay. But the inclusion of broadcasters perhaps requires justification.

The argument in brief is this. In any broadcasting organisation a distinction can be made between management, responsible for the overall planning of operations and the major conduit for controls exercised by the state, on the one hand, and those involved in day-to-day production on the other. When people talk of broadcasters, they often confuse these two quite distinct groups. The latter is in general the source of creativity in broadcasting. It is through them that, for better or worse, the diverse voices of the public are expressed. In the very process of production they are in contact with members of the public in a way which broadcasting managers are not. Thus while a broadcasting system must not be allowed to become a producers' conspiracy at the expense of the public and while broadcasters are all too prone to a narcissistic isolationism and to making programmes for their friends, nevertheless any system which wishes to incorporate an element of freedom for broadcasters, of creativity, of plurality and diversity has to answer the question, which broadcasters are we talking about? It cannot be assumed that the two groups have the same interests and goals, or will respond in the same way to the same incentive structure. This became a key element in the accountability debate of the 70s and, in my view, should not now be forgotten. It is an issue to which I will return.

But let us now turn to focus on the key issues of the BBC, state and public triangle, and the role of the Governors within it. Voices, including that of the BBC itself, are now conceding that the role must change. But what exactly is the problem?

20

At the time of the Crawford Committee[7] in 1925 and the creation of the BBC as a public corporation, the problem of efficiency was uppermost. The question went much wider than the BBC. The inappropriateness of applying Civil Service procedures to the range of public enterprises being created at that time has already been noted. As Reith was to put it in 1966, the aim was

> unencumbered, unembarrassed and unconditional efficiency ... normally untrammelled by any political interference, by any delegacy, by any Civil Service procedures, by any party political expectations and claims, by any demands, by any impatient shareholders – not one factor that disquiets the life of most administrators and managers.[8]

Against this general ideological background and with such a chief executive as John Reith, the rival claims of public accountability were undermined. As we have seen, the Sykes Committee had recommended the need for an Independent Broadcasting Board, but the recommendation was never implemented. Two years later the Crawford Committee, in proposing the system of Governors still in force, also proposed advisory committees capable of initiating research and experiment on their own account and having direct access to the Board. This proposal was aborted by Reith, who set about systematically neutering the Governors and turning them from a true executive supervisory board, as was originally intended, into advisers to the Director-General and the senior management and into a public relations front for the BBC. It was this development that gave substance to Reith's later rueful or perhaps cynical judgment that the system of accountability was set up 'while the watchmen slept'.[9]

This situation prevailed until the time of the Beveridge Committee Report in 1949:[10] in my view the single most important document in the long debate about accountability in British broadcasting. The questions the Committee asked and their proposed solutions still remain central to any debate today. The Committee posed as the sixth of its Fundamental Questions, 'What alternatives are there to competition and to Parliamentary control as the means of preventing broadcasting from falling into the hands of an uncontrolled bureaucracy?'

They had three broad responses to this problem. First, they argued for much greater devolution of power within the BBC, especially to the regions, but also to the staff in general through a proper system of staff representation. Secondly, they argued that the Governors should be clearly separate from the Board of Management, with provision made for their own budget and secretariat and direct access to research.

Thirdly, they argued for the creation of a Public Representation Service to take over all audience research and to become a permanent committee of inquiry. This would be responsible for a permanent review of the BBC's performance, taking into account the future direction of public views on the broadcasting services and the widest range of research findings.

Unfortunately these proposals were not acted upon and the BBC's resistance to them in part allowed an incoming Conservative government to follow the recommendations of the minority report attached by Selwyn Lloyd to the main Beveridge Report and to adopt the alternative which Beveridge and the majority of his colleagues had rejected, namely competition.

Initially the creation of competition let the BBC off the hook of accountability. In the early 60s the Pilkington Committee[11] was so taken with the failings of ITV that it never seriously asked whether the BBC was sufficiently accountable and granted them a second television channel with no questions asked. However, in reforming the IBA and its system of accountability over ITV, the Committee did move the debate on by creating in the new-style IBA a body which did not intervene in the day-to-day management of its franchisees and was clearly structurally independent from their managements. At the same time, it exercised broad scheduling powers and programme oversight and managed the transmitter network. It also possessed its own audience research arm and had advisory committees reporting to it directly. It later developed, however inadequately, a system of public reviews of company performance.

The period from 1968 up to the launching of Channel Four in 1982 was one of intense and rich debate on the future of broadcasting in which the question of accountability took centre stage. And for the first time, employees in the industry played a major role. This period of ferment and of questioning the broadcasting status quo had a number of sources. First, there was the general international climate of social liberation that has come to be symbolised by the date, 1968. A strong libertarian thrust, a general decline of deference associated with the development of vital, alternative cultural forms and lifestyles from which neither broadcasting nor politics was immune. In addition the rapid expansion of the BBC after the creation of BBC 2 had led to an explosive growth of staff which undermined the traditional control structure within the Corporation. There were too many younger staff who had not been socialised into the BBC's traditional ways. At the same time, BBC 2 imposed new financial strains. The BBC's income from licence fees was losing its buoyancy as a result of inflation and of saturation in the ownership of television sets. Consequently the BBC started down the commercial road which has led to the BBC Enterprises of today and to the satellite deals with News International and Thames Television.

It was in this period also that the question of Ulster began to haunt British Television and exposed, as many television journalists saw it, the dangerous state control of information in general and of broadcast information in particular. The sham of impartiality and objectivity was exposed – concepts and a practice which had been used to square the circle between broadcasting freedom on the one hand and political accountability on the other.

To the generally unsettled political climate and the financial strains affecting the BBC and also, for different reasons, ITV, there was added more specifically an internal crisis for the BBC, precipitated by proposals to restructure the Corporation and its radio services. Announced in a publication, *Broadcasting in the Seventies*,[12] the proposals set off a wave of staff protest to supplement protests from the wider public that major policy changes were being introduced without adequate consultation. The same charge was levelled against the Conservative government which had come to power in 1970 and introduced commercial local radio. All previous changes of such a major kind in broadcasting policy had been preceded by public inquiries, but none took place in this case. The IBA followed the prevailing fashion by demanding that commercial television should be given the unfilled fourth television channel, again without any inquiry or public debate.

All these factors contributed to the creation of a range of lobby groups and lobbying activities. The first, created in early 1969, was the Free Communications Group, an *ad hoc* group of media workers, who published *Open Secret* with the aim of washing the industry's dirty linen in public and ensuring that the actions of media managements and interfering politicians should be subject to some public scrutiny. A rash of internal BBC samizdat publications was followed by the creation of the Kensington House Group, proposing a more devolved and participatory style of BBC management, and by the 76 Group, campaigning for a public inquiry into broadcasting. (The incoming Conservative government had cancelled the Committee on Broadcasting which, under Lord Annan, the Labour government had set up.) The Labour government set up a study group on the relationship between 'the People, the Press and Broadcasting' under the chairmanship of Tony Benn. In 1974 it published controversial policy proposals under the title of *The People and the Media*.[13] Perhaps more importantly ACTT, the major film and television technicians' union, set up its own Television Commission to prepare a considered plan, after research and consultation with members and other interested parties, for the future of the broadcasting industry.

Common to all these initiatives was the view that broadcasting management could no longer be relied upon either to voice the views of broadcasters in general or to fight to defend the public interest in broadcasting. A more participatory style of broadcasting management was needed to reinforce broadcasting's independence from government (on the grounds that a large number of people is harder to nobble than a few) and was likely to reflect an increasing cultural, social and political pluralism more accurately.

It was at this time that it became common to criticise British broadcasting in general, and the BBC in particular, as representing the views of white, middle-class males. Thus the movement for greater worker participation in broadcasting management was coupled with demands for equal opportunities, the lack of which was seen as a significant failure of the existing system of accountability, in particular of the IBA and the Board of Governors of the BBC, truly to represent the public or their interests. This participatory thrust was part of a wider movement towards workers' control at the time, and was associated with greater grass-roots activist participation in both the Labour Party and the trade unions. This made it all the more suspect among the managers of broadcasting and the political establishment.

The spirit of all these initiatives is well captured in the introduction to *The People and the Media*:

> Control of the media in a relatively few hands inevitably leads to a closed system of decision making. As the [Labour] Party has made clear elsewhere, we believe in extending the opportunities for industrial democracy, so that workpeople are able to enter into decisions about more than mere trivia. It is important to extend the degree to which those who work in the media can participate in decisions at every level, and have a chance to influence the general shape and tone of the publications or programmes with which they are connected. But it is also important for the wider community or public to have some effective influence over the communications system, and it is important that the less articulate and the less organised should be able to put their views across and gain 'access' as well as the experienced groups. ...
>
> The media are in fact failing to relate to the needs of society. They are not reflecting the wide diversity of interests, but are confining themselves to the narrow middle group of what their controllers consider acceptable and uncontroversial. Thus although we are constantly taught to believe that we inhabit a free and open

society, we have in fact come to live in a remarkably closed system, even by comparison with other countries.

The unnecessary secrecy which surrounds government adminis- tration and the severe restrictions upon freedom of information inhibits the ability of Press and broadcasting to do their proper job. ... Worse than this, our broadcasting structures mirror this closed system of government. The actions of these organisations, which were established to promote the public interest in broad- casting, show more concern with keeping the public at a safe distance. We are constantly being asked to believe that they are fighting a long and desperate battle against government control – with our interests at heart, but necessarily behind closed doors.

It is more likely that, like countless other organisations, they find it more comfortable not to be bothered with holding themselves accountable to public and workers. Certainly, all the machinery so far established with the ostensible purpose of furthering participa- tion has been transparently designed to ward it off.[14]

I have quoted this document at length because it so accurately reflects the spirit of its times and the themes of the debate in the early 70s of broadcasting accountability. However, as a result of the Annan Committee Report and the eventual setting up of Channel Four, this movement for greater accountability was diverted into the cause of the independent production sector and the model of the broadcaster as publisher. It is just part of the recent tragic history of accountability in British broadcasting that many who participated in these develop- ments and fought for independence, however misguidedly, have now discovered that the end result at the BBC, with the 25 per cent quota of independent production and Producer Choice, is that power is more firmly concentrated than ever in the hands of commissioning editors and channel controllers. In consequence proper questions of broad- casting programme policy can be hidden behind cost-accountancy efficiency criteria.

When the Annan Committee was revived by the Labour government in 1974, it became the site of the debate on accountability. The Report and its effect on the question were deeply ambiguous. On the one hand it was reactionary in both reinforcing the notion that a public service is to be judged in terms of audience reaction to individual programmes and in firmly smacking down upstart workers. As the Report put it,

the contention that the overweening power of the broadcasters who set the 'agenda' and 'define reality' for the public and structure the view between 'governors and governed' must be curbed, while at the same time the individual producer is to be granted far greater freedom, seems to us a mysterious paradox.

As I argued in my *Structures of Television*, 'This only seems a paradox if one fails to differentiate within the category "broadcaster" between broadcasting management and the interests and functions of the broadcasting institution on the one hand, and the individual broadcaster on the other.'[15]

The Annan Committee was led to make a harmful and confused distinction between on the one hand bureaucracy, which was bad, and on the other, creative freedom, which was good, leading them consistently to underplay the importance of accountability structures in the name of creative freedom. They stated:

> We do not agree with those who have suggested that the concern of the Pilkington Committee for good programmes was somehow misconceived and that the real issue is the control of broadcasting ... on the contrary we regard the programmes as unquestionably the most important – and arguably the only – test of any broadcasting system. ... Programmes are made by the people who create them and creation does not express itself through the rational application of rules, guidelines or regulations. Necessary as they may be, these safeguards are merely filters in the imaginative process and brakes on the creative impetus.

Such thinking led to the failure to deal with the BBC's system of governance and eventually, as I have said, to the setting up of Channel Four and the independent sector as a guarantor of pluralism and creativity.

On the other hand the Annan Committee did respond to the widespread public disquiet about accountability in a number of ways. First, it was concerned that the BBC had become too large, bureaucratic and defensive in its relations both with its own workers and the public. It was thus led to recommend splitting up the BBC and, perhaps more importantly, to recommend, partly because of the increased speed of technical and social change, the creation of a Public inquiry Board for Broadcasting. This was to fulfil the function of Beveridge's suggested Public Representation Service, although Annan extended the proposal to the whole broadcasting system. The Board would, in effect, conduct a permanent inquiry into broadcasting, both commissioning and marshalling research and functioning as a channel for public concerns about the operations of the system. Its only powers would be to make recommendations to ministers, although, of course, it was envisaged that it would have access to the internal information of broadcasters necessary for its task. Since that time, we have witnessed the setting up of a number of regulatory bodies, such as OFTEL, which at least carry out some of the functions with respect to the industries for which they are each responsible.

The proposals were never acted on. While the establishment of Channel Four, as we have seen, diverted some of the pressure for accountability, especially from the broadcasting workforce, the wider concerns did not simply disappear. I said at the outset of this essay that one form they took was in the renewed attempt to solve the problems through competition. In addition the strengthening of the Broadcasting Complaints Commission and the creation of the Broadcasting Standards Council can be seen as partial responses to the concerns of the 70s: the Commission providing an independent channel of redress for individual complainants while the Council, without executive responsibility, founded the effectiveness of its advisory powers on its research capability to provide independent monitoring of the broadcasters' performances.

But the need to establish these bodies was in itself an admission that the existing accountability structures of the BBC and the ITC were not working. It has also led to a dangerous split between the concern for programme standards, on the one hand, and the broadcast resource management and planning which makes those programmes possible, on the other. Thus, for instance, the Broadcasting Standards Council cannot review the question of whether the regions are being adequately served or whether the production base of British broadcasting will be undermined by the introduction of Producer Choice at the BBC. More generally, while the trend of thinking in the 70s was towards the need for greater co-ordination of regulatory powers in the form, for instance, of a Broadcasting Council with general regulatory powers, the trend in the 80s has been towards a fragmentation of regulatory authority.

Proposals for the Future
What lessons can we learn from this history for the current debate on the accountability of public service broadcasting? The key principle seems to be clear, a move towards greater transparency: as to how funds are distributed; as to how accountability is organised; as to how different viewpoints are taken.

First, there is a need to separate the issue of controlling the strategic direction of public service broadcasting from issues of day-to-day management. Secondly, there is a need to separate from those questions of executive control the question of how best to organise

27

both public views and research on broadcasting into a coherent public input into broadcasting policy development.

The BBC has itself proposed re-examination of the relationship between the Governors and the Board of Management. The Government's Green Paper puts forward a proposal for a Public Service Broadcasting Board to distribute licence revenue.

These proposals should be built upon. In effect I would merge them. There is no merit in the argument, which derives from the Peacock Committee and has now been opportunistically endorsed by Melvyn Bragg, that a Public Service Broadcasting Board should allocate licence-fee money to public service programmes anywhere in the United Kingdom broadcasting system. You cannot identify public service programmes, only public service channels or groups of channels. But there is merit in the idea of a body – let us call it the British Broadcasting Commission – which receives the revenue from the licence fee and possibly other revenues, including a direct government grant, and distributes it across the range of services it is authorised to supply. For instance, there remains a problem of how money is allocated to radio from a licence fee levied only on television. Such a system would enable public service radio and television to be split, if that were thought desirable, as indeed I do.

Each broadcasting entity under the Board's control would, under its own executive board, be entirely independent in day-to-day matters. The new Commission would approve overall budgets, on some rolling basis, and schedules in the manner of the old IBA. It would also agree and enforce broad programme guidelines, again rather as the IBA used to do with its contractors. Indeed the relation of broadcaster to the Commission could well be one of contractor, that is to say, one could envisage the Commission putting its services out to franchise to consortia of broadcasting managers. The essence of the system would be that strategic decisions on both finance and programming policy would be transparent and managers would be responsible for delivering performance to an external body with realistic clout. Perhaps the best model for the relationship between the two might be drawn from that between the ITC and Channel Four: that is, the Commission would appoint certain non-executive directors and the chairman of each executive board, which would also include executive directors.

The membership of the Commission will be crucial. Because government pressure cannot be avoided, the Commission needs to be structured to force such pressure to be overtly applied. In my view the Commission should include one-third of appointees directly made by political parties according to their voting strength, one-third representative of viewers and listeners, and the final third drawn from broadcasters through their trade unions and trade bodies – for instance, PACT could be represented. The alternative would be to leave the appointment of members of the Commission in the hands of the government, but only after 'advise and consent' on American lines by a parliamentary select committee.

An alternative constitution for the Commission would follow the organisation of public service broadcasting on a firmer regional basis, as indeed Beveridge proposed and as the BBC itself has tried from time to time. This would introduce more plurality into broadcasting, the schedules of public service broadcasting being made up of contributions from genuinely independent regions, which by virtue of scale have closer links with their audiences, as the ITV regions have clearly demonstrated. This would allow appointments to the Commission to be made on a regional basis. The problem of making the Commission genuinely representative, and thus with a rival political legitimacy to that of Parliament and government, should not be underestimated. But neither, if such steps are not taken, should the problems of lack of genuine accountability and excessive government control be underestimated, as has been historically demonstrated.

But it is important that the remit of the Commission should be executive, narrow and well defined. In my view these functions could well be absorbed into a restructured ITC with some advantage. It should not itself be concerned with the wider public representation function. If the functions of execution and critical examination are combined, the latter quickly succumbs to the disease of special pleading and public relations, as the examples of the BBC's and the IBA's advisory committees show. Thus, in parallel to the Commission, there is a strong case for setting up a body on the lines of Beveridge's Representation Service or Annan's Inquiry Board, absorbing the present Broadcasting Complaints Commission and the Broadcasting Standards Council. It would have a remit to seek out public views, to keep the performance of broadcasting under permanent review and to report regularly both to the Commission and Parliament.

The unsatisfactory nature of the current system has already been amply exemplified by the way the BBC has responded to the Government's Green Paper. First, the future of public service broadcasting is defined in an internal and confidential process by 126 middle-to-senior BBC employees without any attempt being made to involve a wider public. Once again debate can take place only after they have decided what is good for them and perhaps for us. Then this policy is presented to the public by the Boards of Management and Governors as one seamless whole. Once again the Governors find themselves simply presenting and defending an internal decision. They no doubt made an input, but what input and by what criteria? It would be good to know.

It might even be good to think that the Governors had considered alternative options. Certainly the Government's Green Paper is superior in this respect. Indeed it is an irony of history that, in its proposal for a Public Service Broadcasting Council, a Conservative government has now adopted an idea originally proposed in *The People and the Media*, dismissed at the time of its publication as the dangerous ravings of the extreme Left and as the end of broadcasting civilisation as we had known it.

The danger, if we neglect these issues of accountability now, is that the BBC will survive 1996 in more or less its present form. Once again it appears to be the strategy of BBC senior management and the Governors to deflect legitimate demands for greater accountability and to defend the status quo by recourse to the language of internal markets and performance indicators. Given the current political context, this strategy may well be successful, but it could be a Pyrrhic victory. As we enter the first decade of the 21st century and as the number and audience share of competitive channels grows while the legitimacy of the licence fee diminishes, public service will slowly fade away. It will be deprived of the lifeblood of public esteem and support that can only be drawn up through roots of public accountability planted deep in the institutional soil of our public culture. For without such a system the market is really the only alternative. Given the history of the last seventy years, there is little time to lose.

Notes

1. Department of National Heritage, *The Future of the BBC: A Consultation Document*, Cm 2098 (London: HMSO, 1992).
2. BBC, *Extending Choice: The BBC's Role in the New Broadcasting Age* (London: BBC, 1992).
3. Home Office, *Report of the Committee on Financing the BBC* (The Peacock Report), Cmnd 9824 (London: HMSO, 1986).
4. Home Office, *Report of the Committee on the Future of Broadcasting* (The Annan Report), Cmnd 6753 (London: HMSO, 1977).
5. M. Warnock, 'Accountability, responsibility – or both', *Independent Broadcasting*, No. 2, 1974.
6. Home Office, *Report of the Committee on Broadcasting* (The Sykes Report), Cmd 1951 (London: HMSO, 1923).
7. Home Office, *Report of the Committee on Broadcasting* (The Crawford Report), Cmd 2599 (London: HMSO, 1925).
8. J. Reith, 'The façade of public corporations', *The Times*, 28 March 1966.

9. Ibid.
10. Home Office, *Report of the Committee on Broadcasting* (The Beveridge Report), Cmd 8116 (London: HMSO, 1949).
11. Home Office, *Report of the Committee on Broadcasting* (The Pilkington Report), Cmnd 1753 (London: HMSO, 1960).
12. BBC, *Broadcasting in the Seventies* (London: BBC, 1969).
13. The Labour Party, *The People and the Media* (London: Labour Party, 1974).
14. Ibid., pp. 6–7.
15. N. Garnham, *Structures of Television* (London: British Film Institute, 1978), p. 50.

The Consumer Interest and the Future of the BBC

ROGER GALE MP

Which consumers? What interests? What future? The viewer does not think of him or herself as 'the consumer'; armchair critic, director *manqué*, intellectual elitist, at the very least well-qualified expert, yes, but 'the consumer'? Never. And yet this consumer, born perhaps in the corner shop of the BBC as the sole purveyor of television, weaned in the department store of the BBC and a single commercial channel and experiencing media adolescence in the delicatessen of BBC 2 and Channel Four, now finds him or herself hurled unceremoniously into a real-world hypermarket with satellite, cable and terrestrial multichannel produce.

What are this consumer's 'interests'? Are they the implied interests of the question? The right to high-quality, highbrow, high-production cost, low audience programming? The sort of programme for which it is often claimed, 'Of course, if it were not made here, it would not be made at all'? Or are this consumer's real interests darts and beer and skittles, game shows and stripping housewives, Woe-gan and soap? With *Red Hot Danish* mixed in after midnight or recorded and then time-shifted for the insatiable seeker after sex?

Tied up somewhere in the answers to that ungainly series of question marks lies the future of the BBC or, as some would put it, '*The Future of the BBC*', the elixir without which there will, for some, be no more trebles all round.

Let's get down to basics. The future of the BBC – which is what this whole debate, under whatever grand titles, is really all about – is inextricably intertwined with the context in which any future public service channel is going to be set. So is there a need for public service broadcasting at all? If the answer is yes, then how much is there going to be and how is it to be paid for?

The already abundantly stocked hypermarket mentioned above will, by the turn of the century, offer perhaps a hundred channels of high-definition, wide-screen, digitally transmitted, dedicated interactive channels providing at the touch of a button not simply the range of programmes we now get multiplied many times over but home shopping, banking, education, medicine, therapy and much more. Some of these will still be available by terrestrial broadcasting, but the majority will be distributed by satellite direct to the home or, increasingly, to the head-end for onward delivery by cable. They will be paid for by advertising or by subscription. To these will be added ethnic channels in their own languages directed at the domestic or the European market and further channels directed at Europe-wide audiences as transfrontier broadcasting matures.

'What interests the consumer', if not necessarily 'the consumer interest' will therefore be catered for through every audiovisual nook and cranny. Probably four times the present annual output of 4,000 hours will assault the senses of those with the willingness, the stamina and the equipment to receive them. In such a situation current arguments about coterminous mergers between Channel Three licence holders are likely to have paled into insignificance. Once the regulatory brakes are off, the pressure to achieve economies of scale, if only to meet foreign competition head on, will become a politically irresistible force. D2MAC, the white Euro-elephant of the 80s will be consigned to the Great Space Junkyard in the Sky and the real argument is likely to rage around the future control of a common European encryption and subscriber management standard. (Against this background the question of cross-media ownership will need to be reviewed.)

Advertisers will look increasingly towards highly sophisticated targeting of audiences for their products, making the selling of airtime for wide-audience terrestrial channels very much harder. (To suggest that there will be a queue of advertisers waiting for 'Channel Five' or other terrestrial 'grapeshot' audiences is wishful thinking.) Those who are selling will have the right and the ability to know the names and addresses of the viewers for whom they are making their pitch. There is not likely to be much advertising revenue going begging to justify the aspirations of those who would like to open the BBC to the commercial market.

So, against such a background, what is 'the future of the BBC'?

Those of us who joined the BBC in the 70s were educated in the folklore which has made the BBC a universal legend. Deep in the 30s-style battleship in Portland Place, in the then grimy corridors of the now-restored Langham Hotel and in the hideous rotunda which is the Television Centre, the principles of John Reith leapt from the gloom to haunt eager young producers clutching their copies of the Blue Book, the bible that contained instructions for broadcasting on

33

every subject from Astrology ('to which no credibility shall be given') to Zoology.

It is a fact – it must be, everybody says so – that *Today* has never been the same since Jack de Manio left; that *Blue Peter* really died with Petra, the dog for all seasons, and everything that has followed has been a desperate attempt to court adolescent populism. The news, now read in shirtsleeves instead of dinner jackets, is 'biased' to the Left ... or Right, as one would expect since Players have taken over from Gentlemen.

The mundane reality is that the creeping disease of more channels, first in radio and then in television, and then the advent of competition, have clouded the vision that was public service broadcasting, producing instead a sprawling conglomerate of overstaffed and self-perpetuating empires which owe more allegiance to their own survival than to the public they are supposed to serve. It is these telesupermarket chains within the BBC (with their network production centres) and their commercial counterparts which have turned audiences into consumers and reduced much of broadcasting to the level of soap-powder advertisements rather than the soaps themselves. Under these circumstances there is a rich seam to be worked by those who would abolish the BBC. Why, when a plethora of sources offers a wide diversity of programmes, is there any need to impose upon a public which is not consulted more channels of pap ('and sedition'– Disgusted, Tonbridge), supported by a licence fee they are compelled to pay?

A recent survey will have shaken some egos. The BBC's much-vaunted and expensive Light Entertainment rates roughly five times as many complaints as praise. Religious Programmes and Arts, traditionally regarded as corporate bastions, attract more complaints than praise while even Children's Programmes lags behind the peak of self-esteem that they might be expected to enjoy. In News and Current Affairs, Documentaries, Sport and Drama, the self-satisfaction level (for this was a survey taken predominantly among broadcasters and programme-makers) is much higher.[1]

No clearer answers to justify the BBC and the licence fee emerge from this toe in the water than do from the BBC's own document, *Extending Choice* or in the Director-General's statement made on taking office in early January 1993. Mr Birt said the BBC should be 'clear in its public purpose ... open and responsive to the licence payer'. It should be a model public service ... going with the grain of existing thinking and ventures ... a BBC even more creative and vital than it is now'. Then, 'a BBC which is a better place for us all to work'. Aha! Now at last we are down to the bedrock of corporate thought. 'A better place for us to work.' After years of slumber, the Empire strikes back! But grand phrases like 'even more creative and vital than it is now' don't, as my granny used to say, butter many parsnips. They are the weasel words of the corporate cliché writer. This stuff has been churned out with an eye on the Charter and on 'What we have we hold'.

Read further with Mr Birt. 'We will conduct a BBC-wide Programme Strategy Review.' What in heaven's name have they been doing during those endless seminars that have disgorged *Extending Choice*? Some of us, friends of the BBC, had naively assumed that all this work for the Programme Strategy Review had been done. 'Are we alert to all the many realities in society?', asked the Director-General. I fear not, dear John, I fear not. 'Are we ever prey to clichéd thought or received wisdom or inward-looking perspectives?' Yes! 'What services should the BBC provide for its many discrete and different audiences, of different ages, needs and outlooks?' Now we are getting to the heart of the matter. Do we need public service broadcasting at all?

I have said before, and I still firmly believe, that if we did not have a public service channel we would have to invent one. That, certainly, has been the experience of other Western democracies and of the United States in particular. There are many discrete and different audiences of different ages, needs and outlooks that can, do and will continue to make good use of one benchmark service. In the jungle that is, and will increasingly become, congested with airwaves vying for attention, there is, surely, room for one clear beacon that offers a simple and balanced diet for the viewer who is too young or too old, too lazy or too sensible to want to spend his or her time or money channel-zapping across the ether like a demented butterfly, never alighting on any flower or weed for more than a nanosecond.

The BBC, however, has grown too large, stuck its corporate fingers into too many pies, has sought to expand its fief into wholly commercial territory and needs radical surgery. That surgery need not, though, result in any egghead ghetto catering for only tiny audiences, nor should it. The best of BBC 1 and BBC 2, with the extraneous quiz and chat shows extracted and some sound editorial judgment used throughout, will weld into one good, rounded, national public service television channel. It will provide, for those who want no more, a balanced diet of news and current affairs, children's programmes sport, drama and light entertainment. That, under Producer Choice, much of the material needed will be contracted out to independent producers is inevitable and healthy, keeping the BBC as a publisher in the centre of the marketplace for technical and performing talent.

As part and parcel of this operation, the United Kingdom should embark on a spectrum audit. At present the much-vaunted plans for community radio stations accommodated within the 1990 Broadcasting Act are being thwarted through lack of available wavelengths. As a result the Radio Authority is reduced to sorrowful apology when keen young broadcasters apply for licences to provide their own truly local public service.

Too little attention has to date been paid throughout this debate to the radio services. Distracted by the BBC's decision to transfer Radio 4 from Long Wave to FM in order to inflict on listeners an unwanted stream of 'rolling news', a decision that represents the ultimate in the Corporation's paternalist arrogance, the future of local radio has almost gone by default.

There are now many commercial local and national radio stations supplying news and music. In that context is it still possible to justify Radios 1 and 2 and – this I appreciate is heresy – even Radio 3? Would not a return to the old Home Service – Radio 4 with a leavening of the kind of classical music appreciated by Radio 3 listeners but not explored by Classic FM – serve the public sector very well in the future as it did in the past? And should not such a service be broadcast on Long Wave for the benefit of the many domestic listeners whose FM reception is mediocre, those many whose wirelesses do not receive FM at all and those many expatriates, holiday-makers and businessmen across Europe who rely upon Radio 4 to keep in touch with home?

The BBC must, if necessary, be made to wake up to the fact that many of these people are licence payers, and do have a right to have their voices heard. The News mandarins of the White City would do well to register also that, outside times of actual crisis, a Gulf or Falklands War, there is no great demand for 'rolling news', which, in reality, will mean headline bulletins interspersed with endless and tedious, overlong, uncut interviews. The latter may be good for the egos of politicians and the undergraduate ethos of the BBC's News and Current Affairs Group, but is, in fact, likely to be heavy on cost and short on interest.

A pruning of the BBC's radio and television services would release capacity and funds to introduce a genuinely local BBC public service bimedia network embracing local television and local radio, for which there certainly is a demand. It is too fashionable, in Westminster and in Portland Place, to dismiss local radio, broadcasting's poor relation, as being of no consequence. Where else in this commercial age will young broadcasters learn their trade and cut their teeth? Who else will provide, outside the Metropolis, the truly local news, views and information upon which so many people depend? Such a format would leave the 'consumer' with rounded core services of national

36

television and radio, an innovative and enhanced local television and radio service and, at the same time, help to release spectrum for allocation to other, perhaps community, stations. Is not that in the 'consumer's interest'?

We must turn now to the matter of 'Who pays how much?' A public service funded by advertising is out. There is, and will be, insufficient revenue to support the growing range of commercially based terrestrial, cable and satellite services. Sponsorship is advertising by another name and comes out of the same finite budgets. 'Pay-per-view' would not provide an adequate or stable enough level of revenue to permit long-term planning by the Corporation or investment in commissioned programmes and ever-changing technology.

This leaves the licence fee, although it would be wrong to assume that it must always be with us in its existing form: costly to collect, easy to evade and taking no account of high or low use of the broadcast services. When government finally heeds the advice which it has been given for some years now and insists that all television receivers sold in the United Kingdom are equipped with a peri-television socket, it will be possible to move, over perhaps a ten-year period, to a fully encrypted service. Given an agreed European standard of encryption, it will then be possible to collect all fees, including licence fees, not on a pay-per-view basis, but on a 'no pay-per-view' basis, obviating the need for collection services, eliminating evasion and helping to eradicate the growth industry in stolen sets and video recorders. (There is not a huge market for television sets and video recorders which nobody can watch.)

Such a licensing system has the added long-term advantage that it can be extended to cover each receiver – television set or video recorder – in the home. Thus a family with half a dozen such receivers would – rightly – pay the basic licence fee six times over in contrast to the family with only one. This would be a fairer and better way of revenue collection than giving everyone over retirement age a free licence irrespective of their means.

There is, with the review of the BBC's Charter, the opportunity to redefine the remit of the BBC, to take account of the changing faces of television, radio and telecommunications and to lay a new cornerstone for a system of public service broadcasting that will take us into the next century and well beyond. The status quo is not acceptable and to do nothing is not an option. Equally we must resist the temptation to throw an obese but otherwise perfectly healthy baby out with the bath water.

The mindless extravagance of *Eldorado* must not obscure the fact that without a broad-based provider of public service radio and television programmes the quality of life would, for many people, be much the poorer.

Notes

1. *Televisual*, September 1992. A survey representing 371 respondents: 142 of them BBC staff, 95 from independent facility houses and 134 from independent production houses.

Consumer Sovereignty and the BBC: How should it be Accountable to Viewers and Listeners?

PHILLIP WHITEHEAD

Every idle word that men speak, they shall give account of at the day of judgement – Matthew 12: 36.

There is a deceptive simplicity about the question this monograph has been asked to address. Words like sovereignty and accountability have always been at the heart of the broadcasting debate. They slip easily off the tongue, especially for seasoned consumer campaigners. We are well used to declaring that consumers should be sovereign, since it is for them, and them alone, that goods and services are ultimately provided. And consumers generally reckon that they know better than anyone else what is good for them. Similarly all of us who have been involved with public services take it for granted that they should be accountable, because of the special privileges enjoyed by those who have a monopoly and/or are in receipt of public funds.

In the field of public service broadcasting the issue is enormously complex. It could be argued that the BBC has no purpose without its 'consumers', in the form of its audiences who pay the licence fee. It invokes them frequently, yet it has no direct relationship with the vast majority of them. Between the BBC and its consumers stands a variety of surrogates for the broadcasting audience. The Governors are 'the BBC', but they also provide its accountability to the public. The network of more or less token advisory bodies and direct market research among the audience also provide in their different ways the BBC's sense of what its consumers want.

However, these mechanisms, and the relationships they embody, have not developed as smoothly and systematically as *Extending Choice*[1] implies. The decision whether, and in what form, to renew the Charter provides an excellent opportunity to think afresh about the relationship between the BBC and its audience. That means going back to first principles. This paper addresses three, before

39

assessing what the main mechanism should be for ensuring accountability:

1. What do we mean by accountability in the context of the BBC?
2. Which consumers are we talking about?
3. How should the interests of these consumers be defined?

What do we Mean by Accountability?
Total accountability will be available, following St Matthew, on the Day of Judgment. Most of us think the BBC should not leave it that late, though for some in the Corporation the last trump would be thought of as premature for the schedules. From biblical times onwards accountability has always been about measuring actions against preordained standards, implicit or explicit. In modern societies it arises for all people and organisations given responsibility for carrying out certain tasks by, and on behalf of, the rest of society, whether they are directly accountable to the electorate or to bodies which, through election, can be seen to be directly accountable themselves.

How should the accountability of the broadcasters be judged? One important study of accountability in the public service, *Accountabilities: Five Public Services*,[2] identifies seven main elements of accountability. They can be summarised as follows:

1. The existence of an established framework, setting out who owes explanations to whom, and who are the key actors.
2. A set of shared expectations within this framework.
3. A common language or 'currency of justification' so that discourse can take place.
4. Openness of actions to scrutiny and inspection.
5. Agreement on what constitutes acceptable performance.
6. Agreed systems of measurement to establish whether performance is matching up to requirements.
7. Keeping the financial books in order – accountability in its narrow but necessary sense of accounting for expenditure.

All these are relevant to the debate about the BBC's Charter. *Extending Choice* is eloquent on some of the later points, but it is important to be rigorous about the first element, how the framework is set and who are the key actors. The Board of Governors itself has an anomalous role. The Governors are 'guardians of the public interest in the BBC's broadcasting activities', who have never been able to make it clear where the definition of public interest was coming from, given the arcane nature of their appointment and their tendency to mix management and trustee responsibilities.

Nor is it clear to whom the Governors are accountable for their performance. *Extending Choice* talks about a 'modern and effective system of accountability to the licence-payer and to Parliament', without acknowledging that this kind of dual responsibility may contain its own contradictions, and will cause further confusion unless carefully thought through. We return below to the issue of the framework of accountability. If it cannot be agreed many of the subsequent criteria set out above (and embraced by *Extending Choice*) will remain no more than pious nostrums.

Which Consumers?

In theory this question can be answered easily, but because of the BBC's special place as the national instrument of broadcasting, and the nature of the medium itself, the consumers are more than the sum total of viewers and listeners to BBC programmes. Almost everyone is an active viewer or listener to some programmes for some of the time. We are all 'passive' viewers and listeners too, affected by the national debate for which the BBC provides one of the most powerful forums, and by the culture which it helps to shape. So we may quite properly have views on programmes we did not ourselves watch or hear, which were intended for a different audience but had a wider impact on the society of which we are a part.

Viewers and listeners are thus engaged in both an individual and a collective way with the BBC. As individuals we have priorities and concerns about the quality of the service provided to us, and for what we wish to see and hear. As members of significant groups within society we are, or should be, the targets of particular BBC policies, in relation to scheduling and programme content. Such groups may be peopled with special interests or needs, regional or ethnic identities, or particular sensitivities. They need not be active protagonists for their share of broadcasting: it is their importance within society which counts. The groups will shift and overlap, form and re-form, but they are always an important element in the BBC's definition of whom it is trying to serve.

It could be argued that the BBC has a hierarchy of different kinds of consumers, active and passive. They could be defined as follows:

- *Licence payers who watch BBC programmes.* People who have a direct contract with the BBC, since they pay to watch the programmes. If they do not pay, they cannot, in principle, watch without paying the penalty for their evasion when caught viewing.

41

- *Viewers and listeners of the BBC who are not themselves licence payers.* Usually other members of a licence payer's household, including the small number who listen to BBC Radio, but who, having no television set, pay no licence fee.
- *People who pay the licence fee, but do not watch the BBC.* A special relationship, understandably resented, between the BBC and all national viewers.
- *Members of the public who are not licence payers and do not watch or listen to BBC programmes.* Even this group is affected by the BBC's output.

Each of these categories of individuals may fall within one or more of a number of groups which the BBC will seek to target as part of its national broadcasting policy, by reasons of age, interests, region, race, gender and so on. Such a list meshes with some of the key principles set out in the Citizen's Charter initiative, which includes 'non-discrimination' and 'accessibility' in its fundamental principles of public service, which every citizen is entitled to expect.[3]

What Consumer Interests Need to be Served?
The question goes to the heart of the BBC's mission. It can be asked in the specific context of *individual* viewers and listeners who have a clear interest in getting the highest possible quality of service from the BBC. It can also be asked about the fundamental *principles* which should underlie the Corporation's decisions on programme scheduling and content.

What should the individual consumer have a right to expect? In addition to non-discrimination and accessibility, the original Citizen's Charter White Paper set out five specific entitlements which every citizen can expect of public service:

1. *Explicit standards:* published and prominently displayed at the point of delivery. They range from simple standards of courtesy and helpfulness, through prompt action and redress when issues are raised by consumers, to the deepest sense of serving the public and not merely addressing it.
2. *Openness:* providing full information about how the service is run, how much it costs, who is in charge and how well or otherwise they are meeting their own performance standards.
3. *Information:* the provision of everything the consumer needs to know about what is provided, what is planned and how effectively the results match the targets.
4. *Choice:* wherever practicable, and not simply proffered as an act of

routine, but based on a genuine exchange of ideas with the consumers, in accordance with the Charter principle that 'the people affected by services should be consulted ... and their views sought regularly and systematically to inform decisions about what services should be provided'.

5. *Redress:* so that there is at least a very good explanation or apology when things go wrong, backed up by a well-publicised and readily available complaints procedure which ensures that serious problems are put right, and lessons learnt so that mistakes are not repeated.

All these are principles which the BBC should be taking to heart. For the most part they are not politically or organisationally controversial, but they do require a commitment of resources and a place in the hearts and minds of Corporation executives. It is a matter of regret that what has become commonplace in the everyday language of consumerism in most other areas of public service (and in the private sector) has been so little applied in the broadcasting field. Even in the 90s the BBC has seemed taken aback that there has been a passionate consumer response to its plans for changing the wavelengths of Radio 4, over the consequences of Producer Choice and other initiatives, and over what is widely understood to be the cavalier treatment of inconvenient research data.

The second dimension to viewer and listener interest is, however, far more complex and less self-evident than the above. It goes to the heart of the BBC as a programme-making and broadcasting institution. Just what should the Corporation be aiming at in deciding what programmes will meet the interests of viewers and listeners, and those of society as a whole? This is not an area where the audience can easily become engaged with the debate, because they have only very limited contact with the BBC as an organisation, and even less with the rarified strata where these decisions are taken. Nevertheless we should have a clear view of the general interest of the consumer in a public broadcasting system. It has been defined on behalf of the Consumers' Association:

The consumer interest is best served by a system which recognises the importance of broadcasting to much of our national life, which sustains the highest possible level of access to universal services: and which in general does the maximum to encourage a diversity and variety of programmes of high quality.[4]

These criteria of universality, variety and range, diversity and quality, ought to provide the key yardsticks by which the BBC's performance can be measured. Some are harder to measure than others, and there will always be value judgments implicit in the assessment of quality. But

43

without them broadcasting would simply be what the individual programme-makers and executives chose as their predelictions or pitch at the market, and the concept of the BBC as a unique public service would not be sustainable in those terms. The BBC needs to be developing the most objective measures to ensure that these criteria for the public good can be met, and the Department of National Heritage (and its shadowing select committee) ought to be constantly vigilant that this is being done – without backsliding.

Which are the Most Important Mechanisms for Ensuring Accountability?

In the past, channels for BBC accountability were relatively little used, as the recent Green Paper on the BBC concedes: 'The BBC's functions, powers and obligations have been set out in general terms, in the Charter and the Licence and Agreement: the interpretation has been left mainly to the BBC.'[5] Successive renewals of the Charter have left this position unchanged, with the Corporation serenely unconcerned with the requirements for accountability set out in the first section of this paper. The Green Paper does open the debate on the need to develop lines of accountability so that the public can know what services the BBC is expected to provide, how it will do so and whether it provides them efficiently.

A number of different institutions are involved. There is the Board of Governors, acknowledged to need a revised and clearer remit if its members are to act as 'trustees of the public interest and as regulators', in the words of *Extending Choice*. There is the extraordinary range of the BBC's advisory councils and committees, headed by a General Advisory Council: some sixty-five in number, all chosen by the Corporation itself. There is the broadcasting audience which can be expected to make some of its views known through systematic market research. And finally there are the two Houses of Parliament, both through their debates on the floor and through the more detailed scrutiny which can be applied by the select committees.

Many questions abide. There may be substantial agreement that, if the Governors are going to be trustees, they need a new and different remit. But how are they to be extracted from the confusions of the past twenty years? In that time they have become bound up with management decisions and staff appointments, and appear to have been drawn from a social, professional and political circle which has become narrower, not wider. They have from time to time been involved in management decisions on which they have subsequently had to act as regulators: notably in the case of *Yesterday's Men* in 1971. Key Governors have acted to their own agenda more as non-executive directors than as trustees. *Extending Choice* now talks of separate roles for the Board of Management and the Board of Governors, with the former answering to the latter as regulators. It is less clear about where this accountability lies. How much detail is consistent with the idea of Governors responsible only for strategic decisions? What happens to the Governors if there are major management mistakes (like the recent massive accounting errors) that fall outside their revamped role as custodians of the BBC's mission and values for the public?

The same questions can be asked about the identity and role of the myriad advisory bodies. What practical level of intervention beyond bland comment is expected of or available to them? How are people chosen for them, and do such choices include the abrasive as well as the emollient voices among the BBC's audiences? To whom are they accountable, and what added value do they give the BBC in its relationship with its viewers and listeners?

Only on the market research side can we have any real confidence that there are some existing lines of accountability which can be built on and strengthened. Market research can never provide a sufficient base for planning programmes and broadcast output, but it is a necessary adjunct to assessment and scheduling. It does indicate whether particular programmes have struck their mark with their target audiences, and it can indicate strong consumer preferences among what is offered (though less so about what might be offered in the future, as evidenced by the recent row over proposals for a rolling news service on Radio 4).

It is by no means clear that the Board of Governors, whether retained in their existing form or given a clearer and more tightly drawn remit, can aid the process of accountability. Short of being elected directly by the public, it is unclear how the Governors can have a remit which allows them to define and speak for the public interest. Such elections are unlikely, since no elected government would want to hand over to a rival source of elected authority powers to shape a crucial formative influence within the national culture. If we stay with the idea of appointees, it ought to follow that the Governors (or whatever new name they are given) should serve as *trustees* for the mission statement of the BBC, and that they are there to set performance measurements and reporting requirements for the Director-General and the Board of Management. The latter should include non-executive directors filling the role into which some Governors have mistakenly allowed themselves to slide. Their own accountability to the citizen body could be improved by some open process of selection and scrutiny, in which nominees, all of whom should be

45

required to provide appropriate and clearly stated credentials, could be questioned on their appointability by the Select Committee on National Heritage.

Even such a reform would leave the Governors with responsibilities within broadcasting that would make it difficult for them directly to address the current concerns of viewers and listeners. Because of their fragmentation, low profile and effective 'client' status, the bodies supposedly charged with this task – the BBC's advisory committees and councils – cannot fulfil such a role either. Indeed the broadcasting consumer both knows little about them and sees other bodies established by government – the Broadcasting Standards Council and the Broadcasting Complaints Commission – also carrying better-publicised roles within the consumer agenda.

The plethora of notionally public interest and consumer bodies should be replaced by a single high-profile Broadcasting Consumer Council covering the whole spectrum of broadcasting, not simply the BBC. The Consumers' Association has, with the assistance of Naomi Sargant, put forward a detailed proposal on these lines.[6] Such a body would be completely independent of the BBC, as it would be of all broadcasters. It would be well placed to oversee the quality of the BBC's output and to make detailed, well-researched assessments of the extent to which it and other broadcasters were serving consumer needs, as defined earlier. Such a body would replace the existing BSC and BCC and enable the BBC's advisory bodies (and their ITC equivalents) to be scrapped. Its principal functions would be fourfold:

1. To *respond* on behalf of a clearly defined consumer interest to proposed policy changes, whether advocated by government, regulators or broadcasters.
2. To *initiate* proposals for change, on the basis of anticipated future trends or in response to problems not identified elsewhere.
3. To *research* or commission from others the data on which the above reviews and proposals should be based.
4. To *handle complaints* both from individuals and groups, whether as the consumers of programmes (in part covered by the BSC at present) or as the subjects of programmes (the current remit of the BCC), and to publish the relevant findings.

Such a body ought to operate (at a cost no greater than those of the bodies which it replaced) in conformity with a Charter for Viewers and Listeners, enacted by Parliament. A cursory glance at some of the debates of the past three years – the new ITV franchise system, the amalgamation of satellite broadcasting and subsequent arrangements between the new company, BSkyB, and the BBC, as well as the current debate about the renewal of the Charter – indicate how much a proper forum for informed consumer views is lacking. Admirable as it is, an organisation like Voice of the Listener and Viewer cannot have the influence which the proposed Broadcasting Consumer Council, broadly based and established by statute in the manner of, for example, the Gas Consumers' Council, would have.

A Broadcasting Consumer Council would *not* be a single giant regulator for radio and television. Its function would be a positive one: to interact with a plurality of regulatory authorities, assessing, reviewing, suggesting ways in which each of them, in pursuit of their own prior concerns, ought to be more mindful of the general consumer view. It should be, as the Annan Committee described its proposed Public Inquiry Board for Broadcasting, 'orbital', not exerting static downward pressures.[7] Each of these bodies in turn should be established by Act of Parliament, with their duties and responsibilities clearly set out. In the past the BBC, by the device of the Charter, has evaded some of the public debate attendant upon its responsibilities. An Act of Parliament would prevent that happening again. Replacing the Charter with an Act of Parliament would, as in the case of Channel Four on its creation in 1981, enable the BBC's distinctive role to be defined clearly. The consumers can then better judge how that role is being performed and how a revamped Board of Governors is fulfilling its trusteeship. That in turn could be subject to the overview of a Broadcasting Consumer Council charged with the responsibilities set out above.

Whatever the reaction to the Green Paper and the BBC's own anticipatory document, *Extending Choice*, the time is long overdue for a major debate about the neglected views of consumers in an area so fundamental to their lives.

Notes

1. BBC, *Extending Choice: The BBC's Role in the New Broadcasting Age* (London: BBC, 1992).
2. P. Day and R. Klein, *Accountabilities: Five Public Services* (London: Tavistock Publications, 1987).
3. Cabinet Office, *The Citizen's Charter: Raising the Standard*, Cm 1599 (London: HMSO, 1991).
4. S. Locke, 'Public Views', *Spectrum*, Summer 1991, p. 5.
5. Department of National Heritage, *The Future of the BBC: A Consultation Document*, Cm 2098 (London: HMSO, 1992), para. 7.1.

6. N. Sargant, *Broadcasting Policy: Listening to the Consumer* (London: Consumers' Association, December 1992).
7. Home Office, *Report of the Committee on the Future of Broadcasting* (The Annan Report), Cmnd 6753 (London: HMSO, 1977).

Regulation of the BBC

GRAHAM MATHER

Even before recent controversies it was clear that the future arrangements for the regulation of the BBC would need close attention. The BBC's Board of Governors has recognised that its own role was now in question and that a new 'contract' with the public was overdue. This paper attempts to assess the best way forward for regulation of the BBC and the future role of the Board of Governors.

The Government's Green Paper on the BBC set out some of the options for a new role for the Governors:

> In future, the Governors could be given a different and clearer remit. They would be responsible for the Corporation's strategic policies and for appointing the most senior staff, but not for its day-to-day management. The Governors would supervise the BBC rather than manage it.
>
> Or the Governors could become regulators, without responsibilities for the BBC's policy-making. They might have a role in setting targets for improved efficiency and for monitoring whether those targets had been met.
>
> Another possibility would be to give them special responsibilities for finding out the public's views of the BBC's services, for ensuring that BBC managers are responsive to these views, and that the BBC's programme obligations are met ...[1]

The Green Paper concludes this section by raising and dismissing the possibility of elected Governors as confusing the Governors' role as 'representative of the BBC's audiences and the Government, representing the general public'.

This section of the Green Paper is not pin-sharp. Option 1, the strategic role, is really the existing doctrine. It has clearly not provided a robust enough distinction between strategy and management. Option 3 is scarcely viable other than as a means of pensioning off the

Governors and reincarnating them as a version of feedback-by-committee. The existing, succinct fifteen-minute radio programme, a television equivalent of similar standard, plus the usual survey work and sharpened up management structures scarcely need the resurrection of the former BBC advisory councils.

The Governors are most needed, and most likely to reappear, as regulators. The definition of their role and interaction with other elements of broadcasting regulation, including government departments and the ITC, will be of profound importance, and this issue has yet to receive widespread significance.

In his paper, *Reforming the BBC*, Chris Hopson, a former special adviser at the Department of National Heritage, suggests that the ITC 'might regulate all of British televison':

> There is also the problem of conflicting regulators – the BBC is currently 'regulated' by the Board of Governors whereas the new UK Gold satellite will be regulated by the ITC. Once these problems are surmounted, for example by allowing the ITC to regulate all of British television, the BBC should make the most effective use possible of the vast resource it has. It should hand BBC Enterprises over to a private company, in return for a share of the profits, as a means of creating the commercial culture that Enterprises needs to succeed.[2]

There are serious problems with the idea of the ITC regulating everything. The concentration of power in one regulatory body would be excessive. It would defeat the important emerging principle of competition among regulators. But Hopson's radical and interesting ideas highlight the importance of decisions on regulatory structure. They highlight two existing problems: the possibility of looming tension between the BBC and the ITC over regulatory decisions, and the past difficulties in marrying the commercial impulses of BBC Enterprises to existing structures and control requirements.

These issues will be difficult to separate from questions of accountability. At one level these hang around the role of the Governors and who appoints them. At a second they concern the relationship between the BBC's Governors and other regulators, the ITC and other broadcasting authorities, including a Public Service Broadcasting Board, were one to be established. The Green Paper contents itself with the regulatory aspect of the latter by saying that 'its relationship with other broadcasting authorities would need to be clearly defined'.

The third level concerns relationships with government and Parliament. Here the Green Paper notes that, once a framework is in place,

the government will appoint the members of the regulatory authorities. It raises the idea of a select committee subcommittee to monitor
public service broadcasting continuously and parliamentary involvement in the appointment of Governors, but notes that both ideas could
increase political influence on programmes. It seems to favour some
variant on existing select committee procedures which could provide
an opportunity for *regular but not continuous* parliamentary review.
This seems the most desirable outcome and would be compatible with
loose parliamentary oversight of all broadcasting and not just its
public service component. Parliamentary select committees are not
well suited to the discussion of personalities or the selection of
candidates for membership of the Board of Governors. It is, however,
important that, through a select committee, Parliament should have
the opportunity to exercise some scrutiny of the working of the
broadcasting market and its regulatory systems.

What of the Governors themselves? A number of points about the
future role of the Governors are now coming together, and fit well
with the BBC's own wish, expressed after the debate over John Birt's
terms of employment, to establish a clear contract with the public and
improve accountability.

The comments of the distinguished broadcaster, Sir David Atten-
borough, show that there is now a wide understanding of the need to
establish a clearer distinction between regulatory supervision and
management. Speaking on the *Today* programme, he said:

> My concern is that the Board of Governors has lost sight of its
> original role. It was originally a group of people who represented
> the public interest and protected the BBC against political interfer-
> ence and supervised its affairs to make sure they were conducted
> with proper probity. But they did not manage. The Chairman and
> now the Deputy Chairman have become very much managers.

The preliminary report from members of the unofficial commission
on the BBC's future, organised by the British Film Institute and
BAFTA, also called for more accountability. As the *Guardian*
reported:

> The Commissioners – Baroness Blackstone, Helena Kennedy, Pro-
> fessor David Vines, and Professor Aubrey Silberston – said, 'Gover-
> nors should monitor the BBC, not manage it, and there needs to be
> a clearer separation of the powers of the Board of Management and
> the Board of Governors. Governors must be independent of
> government and need to maintain a high standard of public probity

51

and act in the public interest. Tony Lennon, the President of the broadcasting union, BECTU, accused the Governors of having their heads in the sand and [being] unable to represent the public interest. John Foster, General Secretary of the National Union of Journalists, said a system was needed where Governors were accountable and 'not political poodles of those in power'.[3]

Interest has also focused on ideas such as those of Phillip Whitehead, Chairman of the Consumers' Association, who said that the Governors did not command confidence as public trustees. He is advocating a Broadcasting Consumers' Council to give a voice to the licence payer and to replace bodies like the Broadcasting Standards Council and the Broadcasting Complaints Commission.

My assumption and preference is that the Board of Governors becomes an explicitly regulatory body, appointed by the Secretary of State for National Heritage, which is sharply distinguished from the management function of the BBC. It is clear that the inadequate separation of functions demonstrated in recent years is undesirable in principle and practice. The BBC Governors, as they have operated in recent years, represented an earlier type of public body; they were more akin to the board of an old-fashioned nationalised industry than the regulators of a utility operating on businesslike lines.

The chief problem with the old nationalised industry regulatory model was that it institutionalised conflicts of interest. In this model neither ministers nor officials and board members dealing with industry affairs knew whether their duty lay in controlling management, supporting management, joining in management, defending industry performance, representing the public or representing customers. The regulatory model which replaced the old nationalised industry model has some imperfections. They focus around the personalisation of the powers of regulatory officials, the relatively wide discretion with which they are equipped and the underdeveloped framework of law dealing with accountability, patterns of consultation, appeals and redress.

Regulatory second-guessing of management decisions against shifting goal posts and changing policy objectives creates uncertainty, reduces competitive pressures (by removing the profit incentive for entry) and allows regulators to increase controls. These problems stem directly from two aspects of the original regulatory settlements: the vagueness of the arrangements for the speed and extent of future competitive market entry, and uncertainty as to the ultimate destination of the regulators themselves – was there to be a point when sufficient competition had been achieved to allow relaxation or remove entirely the regulatory role?

But the BBC may succeed in avoiding most of these problems. Because it has not been privatised there has been no pressure at the time of flotation to choke off competition in order to get the business away into private ownership. There has been a greater degree of discussion about the scope of competition in the broadcasting market, and there is no reason why the Charter renewal debate itself will not be thorough and extended, notwithstanding the broad consensus which has emerged about the BBC's future.

Most importantly it has in the Board of Governors the embryo of a regulatory system and the opportunity to demonstrate, in the run-up to Charter renewal, that the system works. During the period 1993–6, the BBC will face a challenge to define the limits of that role. Success in achieving a separation of powers from management and in exercising effective control in accordance with the wishes of the BBC's audiences, but also with a shrewd eye on public opinion at large, will be of the essence and, in this respect, the Governors will be following somewhat the same course as existing utility regulators.

Utility regulators currently tend to be single officials, but it is worth noting that there is a swing towards the idea of multimember Commissions in this field. A recent report by Dr Cento Veljanovski highlighted the risks of single-regulator systems (gas, electricity, etc.).[4] The report complains that single regulators tend to exercise excessive discretion and are unpredictable, resisting the greater certainty of rules-based systems with clear rights of redress. It is noteworthy that recent government initiatives have tended to the establishment of multimember panels to oversee regulatory decisions in water and telecommunications, and to adjudicate cases of alleged restrictive trade practices: these are subgroups of the Monopolies Commission. This swing helps to point the way to a remodelled Board of Governors or ITC which, as a relatively new body, would be well placed to catch current fashion in regulatory structures. It would achieve this through appointed members supervising a strong and technically experienced staff.

It is worth noting that David Glencross, Chief Executive of the ITC, has shown an interest in emerging from the regulatory ghetto of broadcasting and comparing the ITC's structure, methods and approaches with that of other regulators. In the following extract from his contribution to *Regulators and the Market*, he demonstrates a clear understanding of the fact that the ITC as regulator must be at arm's length from its regulatees and that it must operate on a rules-based system. He anticipated rather neatly the problems

53

which a number of commentators now see underlying the role of the BBC's Board of Governors:

As broadcaster and publisher of its contractors' programmes, the IBA has sometimes been hard put to distinguish between the role of manager and the role of regulator. There has also been a sense in which it has been the advocate both of the system and of its contractors. By contrast the ITC will be a regulator of some hundreds of licensees competing for viewers and for revenue. It will be a licensing body operating at arm's length from its licensees ... the ITC has had to and will have to set out its requirements (whether they apply to all or only to particular groups of licensees) clearly in its licences, codes and guidelines, and that these documents and its procedures generally are founded on the provisions of the new Act. ... To a considerable extent the system will be one of self-regulation by the licensees within a clear framework of obligations and codes of practice. The ITC will need to have an effective information system to allow it to take prompt action when problems arise. For their part, the licensees will have to have their own internal procedures to ensure that they meet the standards and requirements of their licence. It will be for the licensees, for example, to make proper arrangements for the handling of complaints about programmes, scheduling, advertising and technical operation standards.[5]

Glencross also highlighted the introduction of the familiar test against measures that would restrict, distort or prevent competition. He said that the effect of Section 39 and Schedule 4 of the Act would lead to a 'carefully articulated sharing of regulatory responsibilities between the ITC, the OFT, and the MMC ... those who predicted regulatory clash have been disappointed'.

Recent events have shown that the OFT has used its teeth. ITV chief executives have complained vigorously that the OFT's findings limiting the length of exclusive programme rights provide

a charter for channels relying on secondary product and picking off the best of ITV. On commissioning a series we cannot take options on a further series. So if a new programme is a hit, the BBC, Channel 4 or BskyB could bid to buy the second series, but we cannot do that to their programmes.[6]

Although at first sight this problem for the ITV companies may not seem to impact on the BBC, it is clear that issues relevant in one sector are often relevant in another. In the medium-term, the BBC's regulatory infrastructure will need building up to cope with these challenges. It should not be assumed that because the BBC's distinctive public service role is now increasingly recognised it will be exempt from the effect of general competition policy.

If the Board of Governors is to achieve a regulatory role that is credible and permanent, then it should, in my opinion, adopt broadly the same framework and techniques as the ITC. If it does not, it will constantly be seen to fall short by comparison and be challenged from below and from above. Its own regulatees will challenge it, both BBC management and programme-makers, whether independent or members of the BBC's staff. No less importantly, only by building a strong regulatory structure will it be able to fight off challenges from government departments and parliamentary committees. Otherwise it will be ill-prepared when caught up in the backwash of regulatory scrutiny of the independent sector. The regulatory system devised for the BBC must capture the Board of Governors' important role in protecting the BBC's independence from political interference; but it should leave to the BBC management, perhaps strengthened by non-executive appointees, the running of the organisation, its succession policy, appointments and daily management.

At present the BBC Governors are at the very beginning of the process. They have expressed, and the BBC's response to the Green Paper reiterates, a desire for change. But as change begins in 1993, it will be against a background in which

- the governors themselves were appointed in a very different environment, not with an eye to their talent *qua* regulators
- the BBC's staff infrastructure equally lacks a corpus of regulatory expertise
- senior management will instinctively seek to limit the impact of the Governors' regulatory powers on their work in practice, however much they may be committed in principle to a new regime.

If the BBC is to prepare effectively, it should recognise that building its new regulatory function may have to be speeded up, so that its main elements are in place long before 1996. In particular it will require a regulatory subcommittee of Governors probably within twelve months, with a corpus of key staff preparing for the separation of powers during that period, and a secretary of a stature broadly comparable to his or her equivalent at the ITC or to a utility regulator. It will need to recognise that Governors-as-regulators will be very much more distinct from the BBC than his historically been the case. They and their regulatory staff, for example, would almost certainly need to be physically distinct from the BBC's management. Their budget arrangements would have to be isolated from direct management control.

Where commercial partnerships, practices or potential anticompetitive systems are concerned, there is a prima-facie case for discussion on a formalised basis of common principles between the BBC and the ITC. In my view, however, it may be desirable to establish either a standing joint committee between the two organisations or *ad hoc* committees on particular subjects, such a specific secondary market issues. The advantage of this would be that

- arrangements would be in place to identify and head off the regulatory consequences of divergent practices
- both parties would therefore expect to face fewer inquiries from the competition authorities, as their systems would send more early warnings
- there would be no compulsion to follow identical practices, but a natural pressure for reasonable convergence
- where difficulties were causing public concern (as in the case of recent BBC trails and ITV rights restrictions) there would be a forum to attempt redress.

The initial debate on the future of the BBC has shown that there is little support for the fragmentation of the Corporation, or for the establishment of a Public Service Broadcasting Council, whose advocates have failed to provide convincing evidence that it would be likely to deliver public service broadcasting more effectively than a reformed BBC. Yet, especially after recent events, a failure by the BBC to develop a convincing model for its own regulation would jeopardise this consensus and would make external regulation inevitable. The choice would then be between a PSBC and regulation by the ITC itself.

In my opinion neither would be desirable. The BBC should move quickly to show that it can create a distinctive regulatory role for its freshened-up Board of Governors, equipped with a clear understanding of its regulatory function, separated from management, replicating the new regulatory structures elsewhere in the British political economy. Joint machinery should be established with the ITC to discuss common principles on secondary product issues and other shared concerns. Such discussions would help shape the Governors' future role and should ensure that by 1996 any differences from ITV regulatory practices would be clearly identified, deliberate rather than accidental or inadvertent. After 1996, this approach would allow a new, regulatory Board of Governors to regulate alone without government involvement (other than any necessary framework changes to Charter and Licence) because government would be confident both in the Governors as regulators and that there was a level playing field between the BBC and independent channels.

Notes

1. Department of National Heritage, *The Future of the BBC: A Consultation Document*, Cm 2098 (London: HMSO, 1992).
2. C. Hopson, *Reforming the BBC: Public Service Broadcasting in the New Market* (London: European Policy Forum for British and European Market Studies, November 1992).
3. A. Culf, 'BBC Governors have "lost sight" of role as guardians of public interest', *Guardian*, 18 March 1993.
4. C. Veljanovski, *The Future of Industry Regulation in the UK* (London: European Policy Forum for British and European Market Studies, December 1992).
5. D. Glencross, 'ITC: the reform of broadcasting regulation' in *Regulators and the Markets* (London: Institute of Economic Affairs, September 1991).
6. Greg Dyke reported in J. Thynne 'Fair trading report infuriates ITV chiefs', *Daily Telegraph*, 5 December 1992.

The Board of Governors

COLIN SHAW

Introduction

It is said that when the present Chairman took up his duties at the BBC, finding relations between Governors and management poor, his solution was to 'mix up the chairs'. As a response to a critical situation at the BBC, it has, at first sight, a certain brisk realism about it. At a second glance, however, it seems quite wrong-headed, although it does serve as a useful metaphor for the confusion which has arisen in recent years between the proper roles of the Governors and the senior management of the BBC.

It is, however, pointless to dwell on criticisms which may be current about the recent performance of the BBC. Instead it is better to recognise that the system of governance[1] at the BBC ceased some time ago to be appropriate to the needs of the country and, therefore, to the organisation which exists to serve them. What is needed is an examination of the role of the Governors now and in the future, and a consideration of how they should be recruited.

The Govenors' Role

The British Broadcasting Corporation was born out of an official belief that broadcasting in Britain should be conducted independently of government, but in the national interest. By this means, it was hoped, Britain would avoid the degradation of broadcasting standards which was believed to be taking place under commercial influence in the United States. The Crawford Committee, upon whose recommendations the Corporation was founded, actually described the future Board of Governors as 'trustees of the national interest in broadcasting'. The words stuck, even though they have never appeared in any subsequent official document.

Time has, however, rendered the words less and less meaningful. The five Governors who comprised the first Board in 1927 could reasonably say that they spoke for a consensus of the opinions then

58

dominant in British politics. The claim continued to be valid through the 30s, with relatively little challenge to the BBC's monopoly. Such challenges to its validity as were heard came principally from those with commercial motives; hardly any open opposition was based on philosophical grounds to the prolongation of the monopoly. The Second World War only served to reinforce the BBC's position and, with it, the position of the Governors, despite the summary treatment they had received from the Government when war broke out in 1939.[2]

The Beveridge Committee, reporting to an embattled Labour government in early 1951, took a close look at the issues surrounding the BBC's relationship to its public, but only its proposal for improving representation in the national regions was to be put into effect by the subsequent Conservative government under Churchill. The BBC's monopoly was not attacked successfully until the passing of the Television Bill in 1954, allowing for the creation of the Independent Television Authority to regulate a network of commercial television stations. No real threat to the radio monopoly, however, was to arise for more than another fifteen years, testimony to the strength of the legacy left by the BBC's wartime reputation.

Little attention was paid during the 1954 debates in or out of Parliament to the significance for the BBC's Board of the establishment of the ITA. Appointed not by the Crown, as the Governors continue to be, but by the minister currently responsible for broadcasting, the ITA's Members were, except that nobody had so styled them, just as much trustees of the national interest in broadcasting as the Governors. Indeed their obvious distance from the actual providers of the programmes and the detailed specifications they gave of the output expected from the providers, might arguably be said to have set out their trusteeship of the public interest more clearly than the Governors' was. The BBC might insist, as it regularly did for several more years, on being designated as the national instrument of broadcasting and to curl its lip at the word 'Independent' in the Authority's title, but the reality was that the Governors' position had been compromised. With two sets of trustees, there was an immediate possibility of two interpretations of the national interest.

An actual clash between Governors and Members over their respective interpretations of the national interest has, alas, never happened. It loomed close in 1979 when Thames Television offered the BBC a complete programme on the Ulster troubles, its transmission having been refused by the Independent Broadcasting Authority (as the ITA had become). Unfortunately, at least for lawyers, the offer was never followed up.

The uncertainty of defining 'the national interest' became all the greater in later years when, first, the Cable Authority (with a remit to promote the cable industry which some might consider disqualified it from the title of a public service undertaking) and, then, the Welsh Fourth Channel Authority were created. Whether Channel Four, largely autonomous from the start of 1993, can be said to fall within the same group of organisations is problematic, but its remit has some at least of the characteristics of a public service organisation. What is clear, however, is that the words 'national interest' no longer had any day-to-day reality as a guide for those organisations. There may be occasions, in times of international conflict perhaps, when what constitutes the national interest is obvious to everyone and so can be the true object of the broadcasters' purpose, but they are the exceptions rather than the rule.

Erosion of the Governors' standing as the trustees of the national interest came about in other ways. During the 60s and 70s there was a growing resentment of the BBC for the lack of any court of appeal to which a dissatisfied complainant might turn. The BBC itself recognised this need with the establishment in the autumn of 1971 of a Programmes Complaints Commission, with terms of reference covering complaints of unfairness or misrepresentation in the making of programmes. Later, following some criticisms, the remit was extended to issues of privacy. Though the new body was funded by the BBC, its independence could be demonstrated by the initial choice of its three Commissioners: an ex-Lord Chief Justice, a former Speaker and the retiring Ombudsman. The introduction of a BBC-financed complaints body seriously upset the Conservative government of the day by pre-empting plans to launch its own conception of a Broadcasting Council at the impending party conference. The precise details of such a body have never become known, but it seems likely, given the then temper of some sections of the Government and its supporters, that its remit would have been wider than that given to its new Commission by the BBC.

The IBA stood out against an invitation to join in the new arrangement, arguing that its relationship with the franchised companies was sufficient for it to be seen to be detached when judging complaints, as the BBC Governors were not. However, under the 1981 Broadcasting Act, which recreated the Commission on a statutory basis (as the Broadcasting Complaints Commission), the Authority and its companies were, like the BBC, brought within its jurisdiction. The principle of non-parliamentary public scrutiny of an aspect of the conduct of British broadcasting had been established for the first time.

The principle was invoked for a second time when, in 1988, a Broadcasting Standards Council was created in shadow form, to be made statutory at the beginning of 1991. The Council was a version of the body whose formation the then Chairman of the BBC in 1971 believed he had scotched with the setting up of the Programmes Complaints Commission.[3] The Council, which became statutory under the 1990 Broadcasting Act, had a narrower remit than had once been envisaged by its proponents. Its powers are limited to matters arising from the portrayal of violence, sexual conduct and matters of taste and decency in radio and television programmes and commercials.

Excepting, for the purposes of this paper, arguments about whether two separate organisations are needed to deal with complaints, the existence of these two bodies raises the question should the invigilation of the BBC and other broadcasters be put into the hands of a number of statutory bodies or even, as the Chairman of the ITC, Sir George Russell, in his 1992 RTS Fleming Lecture suggested, a single body overseeing television? The idea had a fresh airing in the early part of 1993 as a response to the performance of the BBC's Governors over the Birt affair. The installation of such a unified body, while administratively tidy, would always be open to the charge that its existence placed too much power in the hands of those making appointments to it.

Greater democracy in the appointing process, however, might make unified regulation more appropriate early in the next century. Nevertheless it can hardly be justified as long as the BBC is principally supported by the licence fee and carries duties which, with the exception of Channel Four, are not imposed upon the holders of commercial broadcasting licences. For at the heart of the task of the Board of Governors lies the need to ensure that the licence fee is wisely spent in the public interest, to the exclusion of all other considerations or the balancing of other interests. And finding new ways to determine what that public interest is must be one of the principal aspects in the reform of the BBC's most elevated management structure.

The Elements of Reform
It is possible to identify several specific areas where change is called for. First, there are the questions of who the Governors should be and what they should do. It is traditional, and indeed legally correct, to say that the Governors are the BBC. How comprehensive that statement ought to be in the future is open to debate. Secondly, there are issues to do with the links between the Board and the lesser governing institutions in the national regions which remain within the BBC. These should ensure that public attitudes and feelings are better known when policies are formulated and discussed. Thirdly, there is

61

the question of how the Governors should be serviced: should they, for example, have their own secretariat, an idea floated originally by the Beveridge Committee, and considered again by the Annan Committee twenty-five years later?

The Governors: Who should they be?
The original five Governors, after a brief reduction in their numbers at the outset of the war, have now been increased to twelve. In all that period very few Governors have had direct experience of broadcasting, except as occasional contributors, mainly to spoken-word programmes on either television or radio. The principal exception, Sir Hugh Greene, formerly Director-General, sat uneasily as a Governor for a short time at the end of the 60s, his unease partly due to his restiveness at relative powerlessness and partly to his dislike of the then Chairman, Lord Hill.

Apart from a chairman and vice-chairman (a post linked for several years to a holder drawn from one kind of educational background or another), there are the three national Governors, created forty years ago at the instigation of the Beveridge Report. Then there are customarily a Governor who has served in the Foreign Office, another drawn from the trade unions and a third with a knowledge of the City. A fourth is usually expected to have links with the North of England. More recently it has become the practice to have a member from one of the ethnic minorities. That leaves only two vacancies for what might be called 'generalists' and might also be said to increase the possibility that Governors could be tempted to see themselves, in some respects, as delegates. However, they are still expected to be committed to the interests of the BBC, leaving at the Boardroom door any allegiances they may owe elsewhere.

It is open to question how far this admirable doctrine, which has been applied in many other branches of British public life, has been observed in recent years. It is, however, fair to say that governments of more than one complexion had previously appointed Governors thought likely to be sympathetic to their point of view. This tendency should be countered by the five-year term given to Governors, sufficient to take them past the life of a single Parliament and, in theory at least, a change of the party in power. But deaths and resignations, which put all twelve appointments in the hands of the Heath government between 1970 and 1974, or the absence of an electable Opposition since 1979, can overthrow proper constitutional expectations.

If, as the next section of this paper proposes, the duties of the Governors are to be amended, then both their number and the process of selection preceding their appointment call for examination. Although there have been demands for a reduction in the number of Governors to nine – the figure which prevailed between 1952 and 1967 – this seems indefensibly few if the Board is to be anything like reasonably representative of British life. A more appropriate number would be seventeen or eighteen.

An increase in the overall number of Governors would allow the number of generalists to be slightly increased, with additional members being provided from the national regions and from England. In the case of the former, the new members might not have direct links with the appropriate Broadcasting Councils, but be seen as representing consumer interests, which might also be the role of a new Governor from England. At present, some 85 per cent of the population living in England have no spokesperson of their own and, while it might be argued that England already has many other voices on the Board to speak for it, that argument is not necessarily conclusive.

The appointment of Governors, while the responsibility of the Sovereign, takes place on the recommendation of the prime minister, advised by the Secretary of State for National Heritage, in the case of all but the national regional Governors. There the relevant Secretary of State gives his or her own advice. Potential Governors are identified from the 'List of the great and the good', but the individual influence of ministers on appointments ought not to be overlooked.

Finding an alternative system of appointment appears very difficult. To accept the suggestion that the Select Committee on National Heritage might be the responsible body would be to impose an unprecedented executive task on it. However, though the final choice might be left to ministers, some form of involvement for the Select Committee in the initial choice of candidates could be considered. Few people would wish there to be a British version of congressional hearings in their more extreme forms, but an acceptance by the public that independent minds had openly addressed themselves to the emergence of the final choice might be accepted as a reasonable substitute. A move of this kind, with its tendency to reduce the area of political patronage, would probably be resisted by the beneficiaries of the present system, but could give support to a strengthening of the democratic process, helping to ensure the nomination of men and women from a balanced range of interests and concerns.

The Governors: What should they do?
It has been said that the Governors' two most crucial duties in the discharge of their responsibilities to the national (or public) interest were the overseeing of the BBC finances and the making of the most

senior appointments. In addition they have scrutinised programme plans and approved major structural changes, such as the radical overhaul of the radio services in the early 70s. It is debatable how much constructive thought they have added to the deliberations, which have usually taken place beforehand at the level of the Director-General and his colleagues. If the answer is 'not much', the responsibility should not be laid at the Governors' door.[4] They are not equipped for that kind of activity – the business of skilled professionals – however honestly and comprehensively the staff sets about briefing them.

The key to successful change may indeed lie in the wider interpretation of that process of challenge suggested by Lord Swann (see Introduction), with the Board acting much more as the regulator of the BBC rather than, as now, its most senior, and, quite inevitably in such a role, handicapped management.

It would be necessary for the Governors to relinquish their involvement in the day-to-day affairs of the BBC, symbolised most obviously by their responsibility for programmes. If the latter were to be relinquished, it would end a long-running disagreement among different generations of Governors about the exercise of their powers to preview programmes. When those powers have been exercised, it has rarely been a successful departure from precedent, souring relations between Board and staff and not very obviously benefiting the public. Released from their direct concern with programmes, the Board would be much better able to deal with complaints about the BBC's output, whether they came from large organisations, powerful individuals or members of the general public. Harold Wilson's old taunt, from the 60s, of 'Public offence, private apology', would have lost its remaining sting.

Withdrawal from the front line would also enable the Governors to take a clearer view of the public interest as it is reflected in the BBC's increasing involvement in commercial activities. It is not necessary to question the prudence of the BBC's dealings in recent years with News International to suggest that the apparently close involvement of the Board, through its chairman, in some phases of the negotiations may have represented commercial agility rather than the longer-term interests of the Corporation and its audiences. As the exigencies of a difficult financial situation increase their pressure on the executive of the BBC, it is essential for those longer-term interests to have effective custodians.

The Governors have long been seen as serving as a buffer between the programme-makers and the government.[5] It has to be asked whether that protecting role would be jeopardised if the Board lost its immediate responsibility for programmes. There is not a great deal of evidence for its effectiveness in recent years, especially after the introduction of the more audible, if hardly more open, style of government in favour from 1979.

As a result of the 1990 Broadcasting Act, which denied the ITC the role of publisher and gave it none of the powers of advance supervision of programmes exercised by its predecessor, the IBA, the broadcasting companies, as licence holders, moved directly into the line of fire of their critics, governmental or otherwise. It would seem only logical to put the professional staff of the BBC in the same position, answerable after the event to the Board in a more regulatory position.

With these changes, the task of the Governors would become primarily strategic, scrutinising major plans of all kinds, for example, and ensuring the effective expenditure of the licence-fee income. The Board of Governors has recently conducted its own inquiry into the reported disappearance of many millions of pounds from within the BBC through unaccounted-for programme expenditure. However, the outcome of that inquiry has hardly assured the public, which provided the money in the first place, that adequate explanations have been found and adequate assurances received that no repetitions can occur. A similar inquiry, should one regrettably become necessary, would carry more conviction if it came from a Board of Governors more visibly in the business of regulation, and if the publication of its report were assumed to be automatic, except in the most rare circumstances.

If the licence fee is to continue to serve as the BBC's main source of funding, then the first obligation on those charged with the protection of the public interest must be to ensure the proper spending of its income by the Corporation. Indeed it is the existence of the licence fee which is the prime justification for the existence of the Governors. They should be the means by which those responsible for programme services are seen to be accountable to Parliament.

The licence fee provides the reason why those programme services should have an appeal for the wide variety of tastes represented by licence holders and their households. It is the argument against turning the BBC into a broadcaster concerned only with the higher ground and an output drawing exclusively upon material attracting only more sophisticated and, almost inevitably therefore, older audiences. As trustees of the public interest, it is the task of the Governors to ensure that the BBC remains eclectic in its programmes.

Under the separation of responsibilities now outlined, the problems of accountability which have caused such difficulties in recent years would become easier to solve. Each group would have a clearly stated set of functions, with indications, which took account of both the intangible and the tangible, of how achievements would be measured. As the Board's agents, the staff of the BBC would be answerable to the Board, and the Board, in turn, would be answerable to the Secretary of State. The Corporation, assuming for the moment the retention of a collective title for the two parts of a remodelled BBC, would produce an annual report to Parliament which would no longer be a piece of image-building. Instead it would point to strengths and weaknesses in the broadcasters' performance rather than extolling the first and mildly deprecating the latter.

The new tasks set the Governors might well necessitate the appointment of a chairman on a full-time basis. The present requirement is for the chairman to give the BBC first call on his or her services. The actual amount of time devoted to the BBC by chairmen in the recent past has depended very much on their other commitments, and everyone will have their own assessment of the correlation between quality-in-office and activities elsewhere. The emerging pattern of industries apparently deregulated coexisting with regulatory bodies is sufficiently familiar to suggest that a new breed of public servant is evolving to meet the needs of a new situation.

In the future, if these changes were to come about, the Governors would be clearly seen as the guardians of the public interest, with the staff of the BBC as their agents for ensuring that the trust imposed on them by the Charter was effectively carried through. The Governors would have the duty to appoint the Chief Executive and possibly also to ratify the selection of the most immediate of his subordinates. They would have an obligation to ensure that such major posts were open to realistic competition.

Links with the Public
One of the areas in which reform is most urgently needed is the relationship of the Board to the BBC's audience. The network of advisory committees which the BBC constructed over many years looked impressive and, indeed, was often of great assistance, but less, perhaps, to the organisation than to individual producers who made good use of their access to sympathetic contacts at a national or more local level. Anthony Smith has memorably described the BBC's process of taking advice as 'lunching the advisers into inanition', a phrase which has more than a tangential relation to the truth, certainly with respect to the advisory bodies which met in London. The objection to such bodies, where they have a broader remit than one confined to a specialist area (like agriculture or music), is that, inevitably, much of their advice simply cannot, for sound, practical reasons, be taken. Too often papers have been put up to advisory

councils or committees which, though on topics not without interest, lack any real connection with the BBC's current preoccupations. Were there some orderly system by which a cycle of issues could be passed in review before a tough-minded set of advisers, then more might have been gained than was customary at most of these gatherings.

Different in their duties from the advisory bodies, the three national Broadcasting Councils work to a more orderly routine and have positive responsibilities expressed in the Charter. Yet their method of appointment, through recommendation to the Board of Governors by a panel drawn from the membership of the BBC's General Advisory Council,[6] must cast some doubt on their representativeness, if not on their abilities to undertake the administrative tasks in the areas where each Council operates. At least three possibilities exist for achieving this objective.

First, the BBC's present audience research activities are inevitably constrained by finance from undertaking very regular testing of attitudes and reactions among the audience in the national regions. An expansion of this activity is one means of increasing the amount of information available, for example, to the members of the local Broadcasting Council in Scotland and the two other national regions.

Secondly, greater visibility for the Councils as the representatives of local opinions is a further area for expansion, making use of the frequencies which are at their disposal. The BBC has, for good reasons and bad, shrunk from using broadcasting as the means of communicating with its audience in their licence-paying capacities. Effective development of the opportunities which exist to enlarge the public's awareness of the BBC's unique situation both nationally and regionally is long overdue.

A third possibility lies in the creation of a Consumers' Council for Broadcasting, described elsewhere in this monograph by Phillip Whitehead. Such a body could play a part in the selection of candidates for appointment to the Broadcasting Councils, as well as to the Board of Governors itself. It could conduct research, including the measurement of public satisfaction, by methods more sophisticated than those now in operation. It could also absorb the complaints function of the present Broadcasting Complaints Commission and Broadcasting Standards Council. It is open for discussion whether, discharging its complaints function, the new organisation might act as agents for the new-style Board of Governors in a range of more lightweight complaints.

The new body could also play its part in sustaining a regular dialogue between the audience and the broadcasters on short-term and permanent issues about television and radio. The organisation of effective non-metropolitan activity by such a body would be a substantial part of the justification for its creation, helping to counteract the dominance of London in the broad national debate about broadcasting of all kinds.

It would be unrealistic to imagine that such a debate would involve the whole nation, any more than the current debate about the future of the BBC is preoccupying the twin decks of the Clapham omnibus. However, broadcasting plays a central role in the life of the nation and in the serious and less serious activities of its audiences. It is hypocritical to attack the supposed influence of broadcasting and make no attempt to understand it or teach the young about its strengths and weaknesses. In a world increasingly dominated by images, the failure to encourage a greater measure of visual literacy may one day be regarded as a particularly serious omission from the syllabus of late twentieth-century Britain.

Broadcasting's own role as an educator, especially in a time of profound changes in society and in ways of employment, remains grossly underexploited, despite the advantages of cost which it can offer. An organisation capable of promoting and nurturing such a debate would be a constant reminder of broadcasting as a social force, something well recognised from the birth of broadcasting in Britain until the end of the 70s and since neglected.

A Separate Secretariat
The Beveridge Report suggested that the Board of Governors should have their own secretariat. The idea was considered again at the time of the Annan Committee, but was resisted on the grounds that the Governors, if supported by a secretariat drawn from the BBC's own staff, would be kept in better touch with the activities of the Corporation. A secretariat independent of the BBC would constitute a group in some respects adversarial to the BBC and not, therefore, likely to secure ready co-operation for the Board. It would seem, so the argument went, to be a sign of no confidence in the Director-General, the most senior link with the Board, and present at all its meetings as none of his senior colleagues were in those days.

The strength of such arguments must now give way to the arguments of a different age, one in which the monopoly and duopoly respectively considered by Beveridge and Annan have yielded to a clamorous free-for-all among the broadcasters and a population looking for clearer definitions to be given to the institutions which serve it.

The Governors would, therefore, have to recruit a secretariat capable of carrying out swift and accurate inquiries into matters of concern to the Board. The secretariat should be small enough to ensure that it was never looking for work to do. Like the Governors themselves, it would be paid out of licence income.

Conclusion

None of the proposals outlined in this paper are fundamentally incompatible with the managerial objectives outlined in the BBC's *Extending Choice*. What the latter lacks is an underlying sense of commitment to a set of cultural ideals; a consciousness of history, an awareness in more than a publicist's words of the national heritage in all its forms – political, literary, sporting, religious and domestic – to balance against all that is new around the nation. The Governors should hold that sense at the heart of their trust and, to underline the responsibility, they should discard their title and replace it with the more precise title of Trustee.

Notes

1. Anyone writing on this subject must acknowledge deep indebtedness to Asa Briggs for his history of the BBC in, so far, four volumes and, more particularly, for his essay, 'Governing the BBC' (London: BBC, 1979).
2. The Government's first instinct was to stand the Board down completely, but it permitted the chairman and one other Governor to remain. The Board reverted to five in 1941.
3. C. Hill, *Behind the Screen* (London: Sidgwick & Jackson, 1974), pp. 193 *et seq.*
4. A Governor, retiring several years ago, rated, not wholly mockingly, his highest achievement as teaching one of the senior staff to make a decent pink gin.
5. Some years ago, when broadcasting was the responsibility of junior ministers outside the Cabinet, there was an arrangement which gave the BBC access to a senior cabinet minister, such as the Lord President. The absorption of broadcasting into the responsibilities of a senior depart-ment of state in 1974, and its transfer eight years later to a smaller department whose minister was still of cabinet rank, removed any argument for such an arrangement.
6. Established by Reith in 1932, when he called for the membership of the Council to be drawn from the fifty busiest people in the country.

Constitutional Aspects of BBC Charter Renewal

ERIC M. BARENDT[1]

Introduction

Sir John Reith, still I suppose the most famous Director-General of the BBC, wrote in his autobiography, 'The BBC should be a public service not only in performance, but in constitution.'[2] He added that it should certainly not be a department of state. I want to say something about the present constitution of the BBC, how it should be constituted and what some of the provisions of that constitution should contain.

I also want to address constitutional aspects of the renewal of the BBC's Charter in a second sense: that is, what we may regard as the fundamental or constitutional right of freedom of speech as applied to the public broadcasting media. In many European countries the constitution protects freedom of speech, freedom of the press and either explicitly or by implication, freedom of the broadcasting media. This has significant implications for the organisation of the broadcasting system, for its freedom from state or government control, and the extent to which the freedom of the broadcasters to draw up their own programmes may be limited in the public interest.

Of course in the United Kingdom we do not have constitutional protection for freedom of speech and broadcasting freedom, or a court to enforce such freedoms, but, nevertheless, we believe in the same principles of, for example, freedom of speech as those which are legally protected in other countries. One fundamental question of principle is whether the present method of instituting the BBC by Charter, with the accompanying Licence and Agreement, is really compatible with these freedoms. Another question is whether it is right for the Crown, in effect the prime minister, to retain a monopoly right of appointment to the Board of Governors.

The Charter and the Licence and Agreement

The BBC is constituted by Royal Charter, which, strictly speaking, is granted by the Privy Council on behalf of the Crown, on the petition

70

of the House of Commons. Some other public institutions are set up in the same way, of which the most important are universities. Legally the grant of the Charter is an act of the royal prerogative, that is, the special powers of the Crown which are recognised by the common law. The Charter sets out the overall objects of the BBC, the terms of appointment for the Governors and the constitution of various advisory committees.

However, the Licence and Agreement which accompanies the Charter is the more interesting document. It is entered into by the responsible minister, currently the Secretary of State for National Heritage, and the BBC. This is the document which contains provisions about the licence fee, prohibitions on advertising and on editorialising by the BBC. It also contains the power given to the Secretary of State to compel the showing of items and his controversial power to ban programmes or classes of programmes, to which reference is made later in this text.

There are at least three odd features in the two documents, odd for what they contain or what they omit. First, nothing is said in either of them about the appointment of the Director-General, or about his functions and their relationship to the functions of the Board of Governors. The Government's Green Paper on the BBC has hinted that this is a matter which might be reconsidered.[3]

Secondly, the duty of impartiality laid on the BBC is not contained in either document, although it is formulated in an Annex to the Licence. This sets out a Resolution of the Board of Governors originally made in 1964 and repeated in 1981, showing the BBC's acceptance of the principle. It is this resolution which also sets out in very general terms the BBC's obligations to put on a wide range of programmes appealing to all tastes. This itself is odd because it might be expected that such fundamental provisions be set out in the Charter or at least in the Licence, as they are in broadcasting statutes in other countries.

Thirdly, both Charter and Licence contain wide powers for the Secretary of State to revoke the instruments, the effect of which would mean that the BBC would have to stop broadcasting immediately. The Secretary of State may act if he has 'reasonable cause to suppose' that there is non-observance of any of the terms of the Charter or Licence.[4] It used to be very doubtful whether the courts would judicially review the exercise of these powers, although it is now quite likely that they would, following recent developments in the control of prerogative powers. It was also doubtful whether the BBC, as a non-statutory body, could be subject to judicial review, but, again, it is now quite clear, after some cases in the last few years, that the courts would hold the BBC liable to this form of proceeding.

Why should the BBC be Instituted in this Way?

The BBC was originally a private company, a consortium of wireless-receiver manufacturers. It only became a public corporation in 1927, five years after its founding, following the report of the Crawford Committee. The Committee had proposed that the company should be reconstituted as a Commission set up by special statute or incorporated under the Companies Act. The BBC's lawyers favoured the latter course as cheaper and simpler. The Government, however, preferred to set the BBC up by Royal Charter, arguing that incorporation under the Companies Act would have meant that the BBC lacked status and dignity.[5] The reason for rejecting a statutory answer was, as Sir William Mitchell-Thomson, the Postmaster-General, put it, that the BBC would be seen as a creature of Parliament and connected with political activity. But if there is anything in that argument, it follows that the use of a Charter makes the BBC no less a creature of government.

Rather than renewing the Charter, there seem to be powerful, linked arguments for constituting the BBC by statute. The first is the democratic argument. Members of Parliament should be able to debate and move amendments to the detailed rules for the BBC's constitution and functions. The Liberal spokesman, Mr Hore-Belisha, made the point in the Commons debate on the Charter in November 1926.[6] He said that if the Charter and Licence had been presented as a bill, MPs would have been able to move amendments to the clause which imposed limits on the BBC's freedom, including the predecessor of the present Clause 13 (14) which enables the Secretary of State to ban programmes or classes of programmes.

The second argument concerns the BBC's independence and its permanence. At present the BBC is less secure than any private broadcasting licensee. The Charter, as already noted, can be suspended at any time when the government has reasonable cause to suppose a breach is occurring. It is not altogether clear that the courts would entertain a challenge to such an action. In contrast the licence of, say a Channel Three company can only be removed by the Independent Television Commission, a regulatory body independent of government. Moreover Charters are granted for only limited periods, while Channel Three companies were given, under Section 20 (4) of the 1990 Broadcasting Act, a legal expectation of licence renewal after the first ten-year term which they are now enjoying. An advantage of giving the BBC a statutory basis is that it would then have permanent status, until a later government decided to remove it, rather than a short lease with a general expectation of renewal. The change to a statutory basis would bring the United Kingdom into line with practice in Europe. But, apart from practice, I believe that courts in Germany and Italy would find that the institution of the BBC by Charter gives the government, in principle, an unacceptable degree of control and would insist on its reconstitution by legislation.

Apart from the arguments of habit and practice, there are, of course, other arguments against a change of this kind. There is the possibility of taking a step towards a single regulatory body, as exists with the Conseil Supérieur de l'Audiovisuel (CSA) in France. Whether taking such a step has advantages or disadvantages is uncertain, but it need not, in any case, automatically follow.

The BBC likes the present arrangement since it is to some extent able to negotiate its own constitution. While that may be a strong argument for keeping things as they are, it seems less strong from the citizen's perspective and the BBC may be exaggerating the benefits it actually receives. It is also worth pointing out, before concluding this section, that the BBC is to some extent already subject to statute. The 1990 Broadcasting Act imposes on it the duty of providing time for independent producers (s. 186) and also gives it the responsibility for collecting the licence fee (s. 180). Moreover it also has duties under the Act to assist the Broadcasting Complaints Commission and the Broadcasting Standards Council and to comply with certain requirements of those bodies.

Appointment and Role of the Governors

Whether appointment of the Governors should remain a monopoly enjoyed by the government must be questioned.[7] Broadcasting is required to be politically impartial and to present a range of views and programmes. Is there any danger that the Governors will be selected because their views are acceptable to the government, or, to put it another way, that someone otherwise well qualified might be excluded from consideration because his or her views and political history render them unsuitable? And if that is the case, does this create some problems for freedom of speech or media freedom in this country?

I consider the present position profoundly unsatisfactory, even without showing that there is any recent case where a person's politics have, in fact, been decisive in their appointment or non-appointment. History shows how sensitive a business this is: Reith was very unhappy at the Conservative government's selection of a junior minister, Lord Clarendon, as the BBC's first chairman. He would have preferred Lord Gainford, a former chairman of the British Broadcasting Company and, briefly, Postmaster-General, but a Liberal. To move to a more recent time, Harold Wilson took a good deal of interest in the appointment of Charles Hill to head the BBC in the summer of 1967 when he wanted someone tough to get rid of Hugh Carleton Greene, then Director-General.

There must be a temptation for prime ministers to appoint Governors, in particular the Board's chairmen, whom they believe will be politically sympathetic to their party. The point is that the British system does nothing to counteract this natural, inevitable tendency. Other Europeans have, in principle, what seems a more balanced system. There is the well-known German *Proporz* system, under which the supervisory board is composed of representatives of a wide variety of institutions. In France the President of the Republic and the Presidents of the Assembly and Senate each nominate three members of the CSA. That at least sometimes provides a chance of a balanced composition. It clearly does so when, as now in France, there is cohabitation of the parties.

There are two conventional answers to the suggestion that we should introduce a more balanced appointment system in Britain. The first is that it is crucial for appointments to be made by a minister answerable to Parliament, and secondly, that it is impossible to devise a more satisfactory system. The first answer was voiced by the Annan Committee when, in its 1977 Report, it rejected any truck with the German idea.[8] The Committee emphasised that Governors (and members of other authorities) were appointed to serve the public interest, not to be the representatives of particular groups and interests, whether artists, unions or listeners and viewers. That is true. It does not follow that ministerial appointment is the best means to that end. I do not think that, nowadays, ministerial answerability to Parliament is taken very seriously. Moreover if it were taken seriously, we should certainly embrace the idea, now canvassed in a Labour Party document, that nominees should be approved by parliamentary committee.

There is much more in the second argument against changing the present system of appointment. Is any alternative system satisfactory? There is a real danger that a body nominated by a committee of Privy Councillors or by a number of representative institutions, as in Germany, would not work very smoothly, with party politics inevitably intruding. It might be better for such tensions to be exposed rather than, as I suspect they often are, hidden under the mask of apparent neutrality. We know, for example, that there were real disagreements among the Governors when the decision was taken to postpone the showing of the *Real Lives* documentary, and it might have been healthier if those had been known at the time.

On balance I am sure that it would be an improvement to move to a pluralist or independent appointment system. The Governors would either be nominated by a variety of institutions and parties, or by an independent Appointments Commission. Although both contain risks to the unity and harmony of the Board of Governors, they seem more acceptable than the different kind of risk implied by a uniform body appointed by the prime minister.

I am sure that this argument would be much weaker if the Governors were managers. But they are not, as Mr Hussey, the BBC's Chairman, said in his Goodman Lecture earlier in 1993.[9] If their role is to act as representatives of the general public, to lay down broad programme guidelines, to supervise the Board of Management and to consider complaints from the public, diversity of composition would be tolerable.

I do not want to say anything about the role of the Governors, but I should like to make the obvious point that the statute, or Charter, if we must have another one, should set out their responsibilities and say something about the role of the Director-General. This might obviate the conflicts between the Governors and the Director-General which break out from time to time, when there is genuine disagreement about whether, for example, it is appropriate and legally permissible for the Governors to preview programmes, interfere with scheduling or insist on the appointment of particular individuals. At the moment, Governors have unlimited powers to do all these things: a balance of power would be preferable.

Other Matters

There are two other matters with which to conclude. Both the Government's Green Paper and the Labour Party comments are completely silent on the first of them: the power of the government to censor programmes or classes of programme. The essence of broadcasting freedom is that it is free from state control. The legal authority of government in this country to ban a programme or a type of programme which it wishes to stop seems to me a plain and monstrous instance of censorship. The argument for the ban on the broadcasting of interviews with terrorist sympathisers still seems thin and I find it regrettable that the courts did not strike it down. It would be unconstitutional in Germany and, with the exception of Ireland, I know of no other European country where there is a similar government power.

Second, the debate about the licence fee seems to me to raise constitutional issues. The power of the government to determine the fee unilaterally, deciding whether it will be increased in line with inflation or not, arguably compromises a public broadcaster's independence. That is not an argument against the licence fee as such, but an argument against the present method of fixing it.

Conclusion

It is my view that the present constitutional arrangements for the BBC do not adequately safeguard broadcasting freedom, giving too much power to the prime minister to appoint, if he or she wishes, political sympathisers to the BBC's Board of Governors. The government's hand is further strengthened by its powers to set the licence fee and to ban programmes or types of programme if it wishes. The Board of Governors is, in turn, too powerful in relation to the Director-General and the staff.

Notes

1. The text is an edited version of a talk given by Professor Barendt at University College, London, on 17 March 1993.
2. J. Reith, *Into the Wind* (London: Hodder & Stoughton, 1949).
3. Department of National Heritage, *The Future of the BBC: A Consultation Document*, Cm 2098 (London: HMSO, 1992).
4. Clause 20 (2) of the Charter, Clause 23 (1) of the Licence.
5. *Hansard* vol. 198, col. 450.
6. Ibid., vol. 199, col. 1626.
7. In contrast to the appointment of Governors by the Queen-in-Council, which, as noted, means effectively the prime minister, it is the Secretary of State who appoints the members of the ITC and the Radio Authority. This is almost certainly a distinction without a difference since prime ministerial involvement in appointments to all three bodies may reasonably well be inferred, particularly in the recent past.
8. Home Office, *Report of the Committee on the Future of Broadcasting* (The Annan Report), Cmnd 6733 (London: HMSO, 1977). At that time there was more fear of a Board of Governors dominated by trade union officials and workers' representatives than, as now, by Conservative supporters or free-market businessmen.
9. M. Hussey, 'The Future of Public Service Broadcasting' Goodman Lecture given at University College, London, on 27 April 1993.

How the BBC Sees it

MICHAEL STEVENSON

'How can the BBC be made more accountable to the viewers and listeners while maintaining its independence?' This question, posed last November in the Green Paper on the future of the BBC, has been addressed in many of the formal submissions to the Department of National Heritage. It is a question that has engaged the BBC Governors for the last two years, and to which they have given more attention and time than any other. All publicly funded bodies in the 90s are, or should be, directly and visibly accountable for delivering the highest standards of performance to the public they serve, against clearly defined objectives. The Governors believe that the BBC should not merely conform to contemporary practice in this respect, it should be the leader in the field. Ultimately Parliament will determine what accountability means for the BBC and its system of governance after 1996. It is for the BBC to ensure that the present system works effectively over the next three-and-a-half years. My aim in this essay is to reflect on the lessons of alternative systems, to recall what the present system was designed to achieve and to describe the steps we are taking to combine the strengths of both.

The question of accountability goes to the heart of the debate on the oversight and delivery of public services, with its focus on the principle that distinct functions should be clearly separated. The principle is no novelty to the BBC; the Governors first signed up to it as long ago as 1932, in a document drafted by Reith and J. H. Whitley, our second Chairman: 'Their functions are not executive. ... With the Director-General they discuss and then decide on major matters of policy and finance, but they leave the execution of that policy ... to the Director-General and his competent officers.'

But recent debate has shed a harsh light on the gap between principle and practice. The line between deciding policy and interfering in management can be fuzzy; the BBC did little to define it, or to establish mechanisms to ensure that it was consistently observed. The

Whitley formula was satisfactory to Reith, no doubt, because of the potential leeway it offered to a strong Director-General; but equally, it set no clear boundary to the activities of the Governors. This was always a flaw in the BBC's make-up. We are therefore implementing a system which, for the first time, defines and institutes the respective responsibilities of the Governors and the management of the BBC.

Since Governors were first appointed, it has been recognised that their *raison d'être* is to act as trustees for the public interest; but the discovery of what trusteeship actually consists of has been largely left to their own good sense, with remarkably little help from government or the BBC itself. The sharpest lesson of the current debate is that the distinct trusteeship responsibilities of the Governors should be made explicit, to bring clarity, coherence and consistency to both facets of their duty of accountability – holding management to account and giving due account to the public for whom they are trustees.

In our response to the Green Paper we set out what we believe to be the essential definitions of the Governors' functions; since then we have gone further in developing mechanisms to embody them in practice. The very fact of definition has cleared the way for a new relationship between the Board of Governors and the Board of Management, in which the Governors' distinct responsibilities are explicitly embedded. At the core of the new relationship will be an annual cycle of business which lays down how and when the Governors will set strategy and review BBC plans and performance.

The calendar year will fall into three periods. In the first, following a major review by the Director-General, they will assess the performance of the BBC over the preceding year. This process will help to identify the main strategic issues facing the BBC. In the second period of the year the Governors will debate the proposals of management for addressing these issues, formulate future strategy and objectives and establish the budget. In the third period they will review editorial and commercial policies and the competitive environment. Throughout the year, the Governors will review programme strategy in each area, and other issues of concern to licence payers such as correspondence and complaints. The process of monitoring and review will be buttressed by the introduction of a range of performance indicators focused on audience satisfaction, value for money and efficiency, and by the activities of the Governors' Audit Committee, set up following the Cadbury Report. The year's business will form the basis for a new style of Annual Report, in which the Governors give a critical assessment of the performance of management and identify areas where they require change or improvement. This year's Annual

Report is a first essay which marks out the approach; as the annual cycle of business becomes established, it will be developed more fully.

I believe this shows that we have learnt something from the essentially contractual style of oversight which prevails elsewhere in broadcasting and in the utilities. We recognise its virtue in ensuring that distinct interests are represented by distinct parties, and that there is clarity about objectives and tests of performance. Our own proposals can be read as an effort to install so much of the contractual approach as is needed to secure proper clarity and transparency. By defining and institutionalising the distinct responsibilities of the Governors in this way, we aim to translate trusteeship into more effective and systematic oversight.

But this opens us up to a criticism which will certainly be pressed by exponents of the contractual model – that clarity and transparency are compromised when overseer and broadcaster live under the same roof. This is the perception which lies behind two otherwise contrasting proposals – a single body to oversee the whole of broadcasting, and a body unique to the BBC but essentially outside it, with its own staff and resources. The perception has force where the sole end in view is regulation; but, where that applies, it is important to recognise the likelihood that regulation (in a rather narrow sense) is all that results. The contractual model comes into its own when it is a matter of ensuring certain behaviour, in the public or consumer interest, by parties who are primarily answerable to a competing interest – that of shareholders, for example. Here the separation of interests must be institutionalised, otherwise there is a conflict. But so long as the BBC has its exclusively public service remit, its situation is different; the Governors represent a distinct interest in that they, uniquely, hold the trust for the public, but there is an identity of interest between Governors and management in providing the range of services which will fulfil that trust. Management has no separate agenda. What needs to be institutionalised, therefore, is not a regulatory role pure and simple, but the distinct trusteeship role of the Governors; beyond that, it is a pragmatic question of determining the form of governance which will elicit the best attainable service for the public.

The key weakness of the contractual approach, from this point of view, is that it tends to elicit the minimum necessary for compliance. There is widespread agreement that the BBC should answer to more positive expectations than this. Even if an external body could formulate a positive vision for the BBC – and that would be asking a lot – it would lack many of the tools for ensuring the vision was given effect. Our argument is that the job can best be done by a body of Governors, their relationship with management redefined, but acting as trustees for the public interest within the fabric of the BBC.

Even in the changed circumstances of the 80s and 90s there has been real pith in the oldest and most loosely defined of Governors' functions – to guide, to encourage and to warn. No external regulator could take on this role, and it is a crucially important one. As much as management it was the Governors who warned of the need for structural overhaul of the BBC in the face of the challenge of the 90s; and although some would dispute the merits of the particular scheme the Governors endorsed, few deny that the most urgent problems facing the BBC have been identified and grappled with. It is in no small degree due to the work of the Governors in encouraging and guiding change that this can be said.

To take an even more recent example, it was also the Governors who warned that the needs of the public called for a thorough review of transmission arrangements before management's plans for a radio news service were implemented. The example is an interesting one because it illustrates both a strength of the present system and an area of weakness which our proposals will address. As the Governors stand within the BBC and hold ultimate authority, they were able to underpin their warning with conditions which management must meet; it was not merely the first word in a regulatory wrangle. But if their strategic responsibilities had been more clearly defined, and borne out by provisions to review management proposals at an appropriate point in the year (as they will be under the new annual cycle of work for the Board), their warning could have been given much earlier.

The point of my examples is that trusteeship differs from regulation in practice as well as in theory, and that effective trusteeship has sprung largely from might be called candour of the relationship between Governors and management. This cannot exist without a certain proximity – it is both a formal matter of access to management information on a basis of trust and an informal matter of atmosphere and personal contacts, and it is the main source of the Governors' capacity to shape developments in the BBC. Candour, in the sense of a relationship which is both critical and collaborative, is the ideal.

Anyone who knows the history of the BBC is aware of occasions when the relationship has been seriously strained – few enough for generalisation to be hazardous, but they seem to have in common a confusion about the boundaries of the respective roles of Governors and management. Our proposals, resting as they do on the definition of distinct functions, offer palpable safeguards against this danger, and at the same time make clear that the relationship is never merely collusive. Governance from the outside courts a risk at the opposite extreme – a relationship whose ultimate logic is adversarial. The cost would be twofold: we would lose the features of the present arrangement which make for effective trusteeship, and we would gain a new bureaucracy on whatever scale might be needed to secure a flow of information from a management which would have good reason to be more guarded.

This risk would be less under the the proposal which envisages a combination of an external regulator and a non-executive element on the BBC's Board of Management, but here the price is a division of the Governors' existing authority, bringing with it a probable loss of effectiveness. To take a case, the Governors' Audit Committee investigated an unforeseen overspend in network television, and ensured that prompt and appropriate action was taken. An audit committee of non-executive directors could equally have investigated this, but by its nature it would not have such authority to hold the executive directors fully to account for their subsequent actions.

But there is a more fundamental risk in any proposal which sets the governance of the BBC outside its fabric or divides the authority of the Governors as a body. Before all else, it is the job of the Governors to defend the independence of the BBC. In theory there would be no impediment to creating a body, by Charter or statute, within or without the BBC, with the formal remit to defend its independence. In practice, though, a remit is not enough – even the Bundesbank, that model of institutionalised independence, has recently had its ace trumped by government. The real safeguard for the BBC's independence has been the determination of successive Governors to protect it. It is so much taken for granted that Governors shall behave in this way that the rare occasions when they have been accused of failing have been sources of scandal. (The cases where they have conspicuously succeeded are more numerous, but equally important are the cases which have never been put to the test because the firmness of the Governors has been assumed.)

But this robustness has been a plant of slow growth, and might never have flourished – even before their first formal meeting, the original Board of Governors had capitulated to pressure from the Postmaster-General. It struggled to maturity through the 30s, emerged from the war strengthened through the extraordinary feat of having survived at all, and has remained firmly planted ever since. It is the ingrained culture of the BBC and of the Board of Governors in their collegiate aspect which nourishes it. Even the most convinced reformer cannot be sure that it would survive division or transplantation.

We believe the connection between the *locus* of the Governors and

81

their effectiveness as trustees is stronger than has been acknowledged, but this is not a complete case for their retention within the fabric of the BBC. The proposed plan of work for the Board will certainly give Governors more effective means of applying their judgment of the public interest, but it does not ensure that their judgment will be well founded. It is fair criticism to say that Governors have been obliged in the past to rely too much on their own intuitions in this area, sound as these may have been.

For the Governors to command confidence as trustees for the public in future, it is essential that their judgment of the public interest should be rooted in an informed sense of the needs and interests of viewers and listeners. We are taking two important initiatives in this area. Firstly, we are establishing a large and representative panel of viewers and listeners to advise the BBC on all aspects of its activity. Secondly, we are reforming the BBC's advisory structures. As much of the existing advisory system derives from the Charter, the initiative here is not entirely in our hands. Nevertheless there is scope for us to move towards a structure which will generate a flow of information for the Governors on the needs and interests of audiences in all areas of the United Kingdom. The formal structure will be complemented by regular seminars to provide focused advice on broadcasting issues of special public concern.

These initiatives, together with work commissioned from our Broadcasting Research Department, will ensure that the Governors are in touch with the views of audiences in general. A parallel move will keep them aware of particular issues of complaint. The Governors have endorsed a new policy for dealing with complaints arising from our programmes – an area of our accountability to the public which has often given rise to criticism, too much of it justified. Our present Chairman has devoted particular attention to ensuring that complaints receive a proper response, and staff who have been involved in the process can testify that substantial progress has been made. But this is not enough to dispel the common impression that the programme-makers are the judges in their own case, or to meet the more exacting standards set out for public services in the Citizen's Charter.

The new policy has two aspects, reflecting the distinction between the Governors, who are the guarantors of the editorial standards we apply, and management, who are answerable for their application. On the management side, complainants will have the opportunity of writing to a named senior official, placed outside the programme areas, who will ensure a rapid response. On the Governors' side, complainants who are dissatisfied with this response may then approach the Governors' Complaints Committee, which will consider appeals on a range of complaints, and require on-air correction or apology where appropriate. The Governors will also receive regular reports from management on matters relating to complaints from viewers and listeners, which, along with the findings of the Complaints Committee, will be the basis of a regularly published bulletin.

It is clear from all this that the Governors of the future will be hard-working people, and will require proper support. Even if the Governors remain within the fabric of the BBC, it is arguable that they should have their own staff, paid for out of their own budget and accountable only to them. There is an attraction in the guarantee this seems to offer of ring-fenced independence from management, but I think it is illusory. We are aiming to institutionalise a relationship of candour; the existence of a Governors' Secretariat, whose principal purpose would be to second-guess management, would institutionalise a relationship of suspicion. My guess is that it would achieve much of the effect of extracting the Governors from the fabric of the BBC (though without the trouble of moving the furniture) and that its terminus would be the replacement of trusteeship with regulation. In any case licence payers deserve to be convinced of the positive virtues of a Governors' Secretariat before being asked to foot the bill for such duplication.

Even loosely defined as it has been, the relationship of professional broadcasters and non-professional trustees, the second with clear authority over the first, has proved itself over time in ways which future developments should not ignore. Many would agree that, whatever its faults, the BBC has by and large developed services that meet the needs and interests of the licence payer, complementing rather than replicating commercial services and giving due weight to programme quality in comparison with audience size. Most would accept that few, if any, broadcasters elsewhere have preserved such a measure of independence from external pressure, whether commercial or political. This is either a happy accident or an indication that the fundamentals of the BBC governance have been appropriate to their circumstances.

Naturally we prefer the second explanation. The present system of accountability has proven strengths, which cannot easily be reproduced. We are consolidating these strengths in a range of practical reforms. The system was designed many years ago to put the public interest at the centre of the BBC's affairs. The changes we are making respond to a modern understanding of the public's right to shape their institutions. If successful, they will set the licence payer at the heart of an accountable BBC – a BBC which is sensitive to the licence payer's needs and interests because it has more fully understood what those needs and interests are.